1

BREAK GLASS

In Case of Genocide Break Glass – How We End Genocidal Indifference.

By

RICHARD C. O'BRIEN

Edited by

Alice Peck

Contributions by: Sasha Taurke:
Father's Arrest in the Middle of the Night.

Special Thank You for Extended Quotation:
Danny Smith: *Wallenberg*
Christopher Browning: *Ordinary Men.*

Photo Credit and Thank You: armeniapedia.org, Nella Questione Armena, Padua, Italy 1962, Saharatribune.com and Steve Halperson. Photo enhancement by Remini Enhancement.

www.jenoco.org

BREAK GLASS

In Case of Genocide Break Glass – How We End Genocidal Indifference.

By

RICHARD C. O'BRIEN

DEDICATION

I dedicate this book to the millions and millions of people who had their lives cruelly and unfairly taken from them and their families that suffered their loss.

I dedicate this work to the heroes who combat genocide, human rights violations, starvation, famine and those who are practitioners of conflict prevention, intervention and resolution, wherever you are, near and far.

I also, of course, dedicate this work to my parents John and Susan who taught me the lesson of exercising moral imperative through action, and my children, Annalise and John, who stole my heart.

Lastly, and not unimportantly, I dedicate this book to you, the reader. I hope this book inspires you to go out and do something meaningful and impactful. You are humanity's best hope. It is my hope that there are those among you who will start anew the next generation of genocide prevention, or famine prevention, or conflict prevention work. Godspeed.

- Richard O'Brien, At a
  Starbucks, DMV.
  August 2023.

Break Glass Contents: In Case of Genocide Break Glass - How We End Genocidal Indifference.

CHAPTER ONE:

"HELP US WE ARE BEING MASSACRED."

The following was the first action the Center for the Prevention of Genocide took during an ongoing massacre.

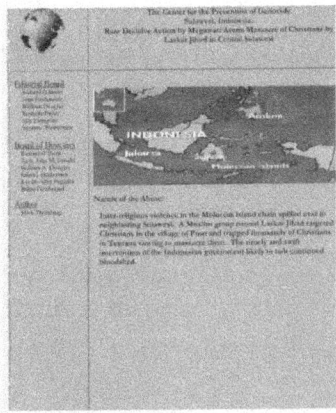

"Help Us We Are Being Massacred." - Sulawesi, Indonesia.

It was exactly 1:45 am when I noticed the newly arrived email; it caught my attention immediately with the title 'Help us we are being massacred.' As I quickly read the email, I realized that all of the theory behind our center was about to be put into practice. The email told how at that moment on the opposite end of the world, villagers were running with children and belongings in hand from the smoldering ruins of the villages near Poso, on the Island of Sulawesi, Indonesia. 'Our coffee was from Sulawesi' I thought. Some of the villagers of Poso had not been as fortunate as those who were seeking to reach the protection of the larger township of Tentena. Swift on their trail, leaving bodies and devastation, raping and pillaging like a scene out of medieval times, were the Laskar Jihad warriors who had sworn revenge on the Christian population of Sulawesi in retribution for Christian attacks on Muslims the year before in the Moluccas Islands.

The email was from a priest I would get to know better before he was to die, as well as two other witnesses to the horror that was speeding through the tropical Indonesia jungle toward Tentena. They estimated the Laskar Jihad militia between nine hundred to several thousand attackers as they pursued unarmed Christians. When the fleeing Christians arrived in Tentena they found that the township was neither armed nor defendable – there were simply too few weapons. Compounding the horror in the jungle, Tentena was being surrounded and sealed off with yelled promises from the unseen militia voices that they were going to massacre all Christians before Christmas. It was now December the second, 1:50 am. I walked over to the glass framed sign hanging on the wall that read, "In Case of Genocide – Break Glass" and took it down.

As I read the instructions, I realized we created them for a full staff. Alone I settled in to use the phone and called one board member and one volunteer.

10

Mark Thornburg was a delightful and capable young man with a quick wit and a studied Carl Sagan delivery. His voice was sonorous, deep and deliberate as I woke him from his slumber.

"To what do I owe the pleasure of a call from the Center for the Prevention of Genocide in the middle of the night?" He intoned.

I told him about the massacre email. He cleared his head quickly and asked a few pertinent questions. I then identified our two main priorities. First, we needed to know whether anyone else had the story - any of the wire services or major publications. If so, that took the pressure off of us to confirm it and get it out to the media. Second, I explained, we needed to get neutral third party confirmation before we could publish any part of the story. Mark stretched at the other end of the phone and said,

"I'll begin working on the wire services and press reports and I'll let you know soon if anyone has it."

"That's why I pay you the big money." I said.

"In-deed. Georgetown out." Mark booted his computer and began working feverishly to pull up all wire services, AP, Reuters, UPI and press from the area.

I opened the desk drawer and pulled out our three phone cards. My first instinct was to call the US Embassy in Jakarta in the Capital of Indonesia to see if they had any word on the Sulawesi situation. The first card died before I could leave my first message.

11

I worked my way through the minutes on the second card through the Embassy operator trying several different

Embassy officials to no avail. Everyone in the embassy was apparently out to lunch or wasn't answering. The final phone card. After trying a few more extensions with no luck I turned to the U.S. Embassy operator.

"Operator, what's your name?"

"Mary, sir." She had the voice of a kindly grandmother.

"Okay Mary, I am going to have to rely on you."

"What do you mean sir?" she gently prodded

"Well, Mary this is going to be the most important phone call you're going to take this month. Right now there is a massacre being reported on the Island of Sulawesi. Now we don't know the sources who are giving us the information personally and don't know how credible they are so we can't release it to the press. But if we can get a credible person at the Embassy who can confirm the facts then we can release the information. By being able to do that, we can bring some attention to the area and maybe get the right people to intervene to help save those lives.

"Mary, we are just a small organization, and my phone card is literally ready to run out so we need to find someone fast. I need you to put your thinking cap on and think, who can you get a hold of that would be in a position to know whether this is happening."

"Oh, my, this is important, isn't it?" She sounded concerned.

"Oh, let me think, let me think." She said softly and paused.

"I have an idea. Would the Counselor General on the Island of Surabaya help? Surabaya is the Island next to Sulawesi."

"Mary he's perfect. If he doesn't know, no one with the embassy will."

She gave me his number and I thanked her. I immediately called Counselor General Robert Pollard on the island of Surabaya and his secretary answered promptly. He was out but would be back in five minutes. I had eight minutes left on the card. In five minutes sharp I called back. 'Oh yes, you just caught him, he was just leaving for his home.' Call him on the other line, she gave me that number – now with the connection fee I would have two or three minutes to confirm the facts with him.

"Yes, Robert Pollard here." His accent sounded more British than American. I introduced myself briefly and gave him the information we had and asked him what, specifically, could he confirm? He thought for a moment, then said,

"Well, yes, that's pretty much accurate. Your figures are a little off though. There aren't 90,000 Christians trapped there, only about 45,000. Yes, they are surrounded and unarmed. Yes, there was a massacre near Poso and other villages in the area and a responsible guesstimate of the

13

number of Laskar Jihad warriors is between nine-hundred and two thousand. But I must tell you we are swamped here because of the flow of people and information, lots of inquiries about the situation because of friends and relatives in jeopardy. So much so I have to leave the office to write up this report to get it back to the States."

I thanked him and the line went dead. The card had just run out. But we had our confirmation. By the skin on our teeth we had it! In a few minutes Mark was back on the phone with me. No one had news of the massacre or the trapped civilians. No wire services. No print media. No one. We were among the first in the world to know. Now, with our limited personnel and resources – who, in the world, do we tell?

* * *

John Heidenrich's voice cracked with sleep and he sounded irritable.

"Okay, okay, give me a second to think." He groused.

I repeated my question, slower.

"Who, with our limited means, should we give the information to? No one stateside is open for business; Europe wouldn't be open for a couple of hours. Our value now is based on getting the information to the right people, but who?"

"I've got it." He said, "The Australians! They have a strategic interest. They have even deployed troops to East Timor."

He was right, as he should be; John was the only member of our board of directors who had written an entire book on genocide prevention. He had also run a subcontracted early warning system for the State Department during its brief existence. The company he worked for, Open Source Solutions, won the contract by going up against some of the US government's best researchers. A well-known Cabinet secretary challenged Open Source Solutions to find all they could on the Internet on a particular country - Burundi. The Internet was Open Sources bread and butter search vehicle. If they produced better research than the government agency within 24 hours, they would be awarded the contract. They buried the government agency in research and were promptly awarded the subcontract for a little less than two years.

John's Russian-born wife was woken by the call so he begged off.

Mark and I began the arduous task of emailing and faxing every single major radio station, TV station and print media in Australia. We began with ABC radio of Australia. I faxed copy after copy of the press release to the scores of media outlets and he emailed them. The fax machine jammed several times before it would allow me to finish the job.

It was an hour later that Mark called me out of breath with the news. ABC Radio of Australia had broken the story using largely our text. Shortly after ABC Radio of Australia broke the story, the wire services around the world picked it up.

We had confirmed the information with a neutral third party. We had released it to the proper media outlet and the wire picked it up. So far so good, but now for the hard part, we needed to find someone on Capitol Hill who would do something about it.

*   *   *

Mark and I, looking slightly haggard, greeted the first interns who arrived at the Center at 9:00am. We herded them into the boardroom to prep them for Capitol Hill. We set up

maps and made copies of the original report, press releases and the wire service reports. Over the next hour each of the volunteers was taught the facts and the background information. The materials were stacked in neat piles on the oversized thick wooden table and placed into packets for Capitol Hill. We painstakingly redacted the contact names and email addresses with black magic marker from each document. We drew up a plan to go to every office on the House side of the Capitol that sat on the Human Rights Caucus and the Appropriation Committee. We were to concentrate on the conservative members. We felt strongly that if the situation were to be resolved, a conservative Christian Coalition supported member of the U.S. House of Representatives, someone the President, George W. Bush, would listen to, and needed to be convinced of the urgency. They needed to feel outraged that Indonesia was about to receive a major military hardware aid package from the U.S. while Christians were being massacred there. That Representative needed to call the White House, possibly the President himself, who would then need to call President Megawati of Indonesia to voice the Administration's concerns about Christians being massacred and remind her of the impending aid. There was a massive

16

disbursement of military hardware about to occur within three months and the over one hundred million dollars' worth of aid might be in jeopardy, it could be argued, if Indonesia continued to allow its Christians to be massacred. The U.S was concurrently fighting another 'Jihad' in Afghanistan against the Taliban at the time. This was clearly something that could be leveraged to get a response to help the people trapped in Tentena. Could Indonesia's President Megawati be urged to deploy the military to stop the killing in Tentena?

I sat outside U.S. Congressman Ballenger's office for fifteen minutes when he walked in.

"Y' here for me?" Asked a sixty something unpresuming man.

"Yessir." Without hesitating.

"C'mon in."

His office was a standard Congressional Office with nicely upholstered chairs, a rich wooden coffee table, ornamental molding on the walls and an impressive looking, leather inlay mahogany desk. There was a framed photo of a factory on the wall next to his desk. He was friendly in a folksy Southern way. I gave him a compelling but brief history of the conflict and the immediate jeopardy these people were facing. I handed him the firsthand information and the Center's Moluccas report. A look of condescension came across his face. He lowered his voice in a conspiratorial tone.

17

"You know who loves this kinda stuff, Tom Lantos and Cynthia McKinney, those liberals just love this stuff." He pushed the report back across the table at me.

"I'll get you their chiefs of staffs names and numbers." He assured me. I knew that the opportunity to get this done was slipping through my hands. He was my tenth office and he was the perfect person to get this done. This was no time for fear or politeness. I had to hit him head on or lose him.

"Congressman Ballenger, with all due respect, I didn't come here to see Mr. Lantos or Ms. McKinney. I came here specifically to see you. You have a strong and devout Christian population in your district. Your district and the Christian Coalition, I'm sure care deeply about Christians being massacred and I know that they would be impressed that you cared enough to pick up the phone and get the ball moving with the administration." I stopped talking and looked at him. The time ticked away and he looked at me.

Slowly, with a slightly sardonic expression on his face, he reached for the report again.

"Now where exactly is this place again?"

* * *

At the end of two days' effort we had seen senior staff, human rights liaisons and members of Congress themselves in dozens of offices on the Human Rights Caucus. By the end of our second day our reason to advocate had ceased to exist.
President Megawati had sent the troops in to rescue the Christians. Within 48 hours of the first report of trouble on

Sulawesi, Indonesia dispatched 4,000 troops to Tentena to protect the Christians in danger. The troops arrived and quickly dispersed the members of Laskar Jihad with hardly a shot fired. The threat vanished into thin air. Within one year the head of Laskar Jihad would be behind bars and the history of massacre and counter massacre between the Muslim and Christian population was to cease.

We didn't know for sure if Congressman Ballenger made the call after giving us assurances, or if another one of the Congressional offices we contacted that day made the call, or if President Megawati decided to send troops on her own. We had confirmed it, put the word out to the press and pressured Congress to have the administration pressure President Megawati when no one else appeared to be working on it. It seemed to us that our first attempt into human rights early warning had yielded some impressive results. This was the first time in modern Indonesian history when the government had acted with decisive commitment to human rights by dispatching the troops. We were amazed.

For four years the Center for the Prevention of Genocide (C.P.G) provided timely early warning information from genocidal hotspots around the world for four years. It rang the warning bell regarding massacres in DR Congo, Uganda, Sudan, Colombia, India, Indonesia and many other places where there was imminent danger to unarmed civilian populations. In 2004, after four years, we closed our doors just after we began to issue warnings about a little known place called Darfur, Sudan.

The C.P.G's successful creation of an early warning system that told of these unfolding danger zones around the world underscores the fact that early warning systems work. If an understaffed and under-funded group could take this mission and have relative success, imagine what can be done at the national or international level. The UN currently has a 'Special Advisor' on genocide prevention, Adama Dieng. Three of his people work on early warning. He has quite a difficult mission in front of him. His office lacks funding, resources, personnel, a clear mission and a standing intervention force for deployment to where civilians are being massacred. There is nothing more important in the world than addressing this unfinished business.

Introduction

This world has seen genocide centuries and millennia before it was given a name. In ancient times, entire tribes and races were decimated by growing empires the world over. No continent was immune to these early acts of genocide – the killing of an ethnic, religious, racial or national group. Even famed figures like Caesar were known to their contemporaries for destroying entire tribes. The Middle-Ages were no exception as Mesoamerican tribes enslaved competing tribes and Genghis Khan famously declared against resisting towns that 'no one should be spared except children under the size of an ox-cart wheel.' But of all the Centuries, ancient and current, this past Century is one of the bloodiest of all time. There are many reasons for this – among them are the improvement of the technologies of war, the proliferation of weapons and nationalism. The obvious dangers of nationalism are well known – with total warfare and industrialized genocide at the top the list. On one hand, nationalism is a man-made phenomenon that we, as individuals, are usually proud of. It is an effective organizational tool for economic productivity and safety. We often consider our national affiliation as part of our identity as well as our ethnic, religious and tribal affiliations. We usually feel a particular bond with the people in our group to which 'we belong.' But there is a subtle danger of nationalism that enables and emboldens genocidaires the world over and is as dangerous as any weapon. The subtle danger is that, while it makes us closer to a comparatively small number of people, *it allows us to assign a lesser station of humanity to those who are not our nationality, ethnicity, race or religion*. It allows us to turn a blind eye to the suffering of others due to a

21

lack of strategic interest, proximity to our group and a lack of connection, and thus it reduces the moral imperative to act. Potential genocidaires know the world community is unlikely to respond if those being targeted have nothing anyone wants. Ask yourself, if a criminal knows there will be no consequences for their actions, how can we reasonably expect his criminal conduct to desist?

It is also true that when impending, preventable disasters happen in places around the world to people who have no relation or connection to you or your self-interest, the likelihood of your intervention in their plight decreases geometrically. This phenomenon has been consistent for at least the past one hundred years.

This book focuses more on recent genocide-prevention action and a prescription to end genocide and less on the history of the past one-hundred years of genocide. No book can cover it all. There are stories, lives and heroism that will remain lost forever. This book begins with a look at genocide over the past century. It gives examples of the cruelty, the misery, the indifference and the heroism of the human condition. It is a clear call for investment in prevention strategies and the organizations that sponsor them. The lessons of early warning and response has eluded our policymakers as we veer from one preventable man-made catastrophe to another.

This book also contains a second book, a manual. These are the first-hand documents from the Center for the Prevention of Genocide. It outlines what to consider if you ever start a human rights NGO and how to go about it. It is thorough. It covers everything from how to advocate on the phone, to writing a press release, to building a communications network of hundreds of sources. It even includes personnel documents you will need if you ever get serious about starting an NGO. It is my greatest wish that at some point the Center be restarted and its life-saving mission continued. But whether it is genocide-prevention or some other worthy cause, the manual can be of use to you.

My personal interest in genocide grew into a thesis for college and a deeply held conviction that genocide is preventable. While the stories featured in these pages depict heroic efforts to save victims are inspiring, the other side of the story, the cruelty of man, made me conclude that institutionalized early warning and reaction were necessary to anticipate the latter. The heroism which occurs during genocide is the band aid, the temporary solution. The remedy that will cure this sick part of the human condition is early warning and response.

A powerful nation possesses sufficient strength to defend itself from threats of excessive external or internal nationalism. But in countries where groups are excluded from the protection of the state, these defenseless minorities are often at the mercy of forces armed with unlimited cruelty. When genocidal abuse occurs in these situations, it is essential that other nations step in for the sake of the at-risk humanity. This is an issue of the highest moral order. Failure to intervene in genocidal activities has allowed the massacre of families, villages and entire peoples, while those of us in the rest of the world sit as quiet observers and subtle, unwitting accomplices.

Because genocide usually occurs in places where few, if any, people and nations have an interest, a mechanism to prevent and intervene must be created. If we take into account that the human condition can be as vile and mean as it can be heroic and graceful, we must anticipate and resolve these inevitabilities long before they occur. The current uncoordinated, ad-hoc strategy of the international community when faced with unfolding acts of genocide is not a substitute for early warning and early action. When the time for heroism is at hand and a person must risk his or her life to save others, by that time we, the world community, have failed to do our job.

This book provides examples of how the responses to genocide are varied and span the breadth of human compassion. The main body of the book chronicles recent examples of successful actions by the Center for the Prevention of Genocide and the international community to end genocide after it has already started. These chapters can be instructive for policy makers, governments and agencies in the creation of an early warning system to end genocide. The group of young human rights activists I was privileged to know, helped attempt to prevent genocide from 2000 – 2004 at the Center for the Prevention of Genocide (CPG), where I served as Director. Many of them have gone on to successful careers in the U.S. State Department, as Deputy U.S. Attorney Generals, Non-Profit executives and fundraisers and one even became a popular pop star in Russia. After the brief historical narrative, we pick up, chronologically, with the work and action from the founding of the CPG in 2000.

In Case of Genocide – Break Glass *Abridged* is *actual* book about the CPG, genocide prevention work and concludes by recommending sound strategies for ending genocide throughout the world. The theme of this entire work is that *genocide is preventable.* Absolutely and categorically, it can be eradicated from the human condition. Successful genocide prevention work has occurred in Eastern D.R. Congo, Sudan,

Indonesia and Gujarat, India and these examples can serve as templates for future successful prevention in the future. Moreover, I recommend a combination of institutionalized early warning and rapid response, multi-track diplomacy, democracy-building and EU lessons from Jean Monnet as a specific prescription for ending genocide in our lifetimes.

The Unabridged, longer version of this book is not the issue you are holding, That version includes an actual Genocide Prevention Manual and has crucial instructions and information for how to run a life-saving early warning system. Included are templates that we used at the CPG for: on-the-ground fact finding, report writing, and dissemination and advocacy to policymakers. The premise here is that almost anyone can undertake to gather this kind of information, confirm and publish it and put it into the right hands in an attempt to end the killing. By placing these tools in the reader's hands, the work of the former CPG staff and volunteers had the potential to keep saving lives.

The human condition is complex. Unfortunately, as much as heroism is part of human nature, so too is criminal or evil conduct, and so too is indifference. Take, for example, some of the fascist leaders during the Holocaust, who stepped in to prevent Jews from being sent to the concentration camps. These figures, who allied themselves with Hitler's Third Reich, and often committed numerous evil acts, sometimes intervened to stop the killing. The dictators' Mussolini of Italy and King Boris of Bulgaria were known to have slowed and stopped the deportation of Jews in their countries. Even in a place as synonymous with evil as the gas chambers of Auschwitz, when a sixteen year old girl survived the zyklon B poison and sat bewildered, naked and covered with a blanket in the SS officer's kitchen, these same SS monsters, flitted around her providing soup and trying to figure out how to let her live. At some basic place in their humanity, beyond the dogma, and the routinization of the task, these men who had become monsters, briefly, became fathers and brothers again. How do we change from people with some sense of basic morality to indifferent bystanders or even, the criminals themselves? Time and again our species has shown an unbelievable propensity to kill unarmed minorities, usually women and children, for ethnic, national, religious, racial and ideological pretenses, while the rest of us usually did nothing. What makes people kill unarmed civilians, when every natural instinct should tell us it is wrong? And what makes most of us do nothing about it? Lastly and most importantly, what can be done to permanently end this conduct among our species?

* * *

A friend of mine, Aeon, observed that we are in the 21st Century using the 18th Century craft of diplomacy. There is truth in this. We have at our disposal the means for solving most conflict in the world, but we choose not to use them. Instead we rely on high tension, time-honored methods where national leaders meet and bargain for a perceived public advantage in their dispute. This antiquated method has mixed results. Today, there are other truly modern and very effective options; there are trained cadres of professionals who are engaged in diplomacy and conflict prevention at the first track (governmental), through to the twelve tracks of multi-track diplomacy. There is the School for Conflict Analysis and

Resolution at George Mason University, the Munk School at the University of Toronto, and the Institute for Multi-Track Diplomacy which are contributing to cutting edge strategies for peace and conflict resolution that can affect people around the world. The usefulness of these norms and strategies, which are only in their first and second generations of development, is rarely noticed. These conflict prevention practitioners are an unknown cadre, often braving places most of us would not dream to venture. They are the warriors for peace, and they are largely unknown. They are a fundamental element for good and they are just beginning to be used in U.S foreign and worldwide foreign policy. Their field of conflict-prevention needs to become the norm of how we solve the problems of the world.

While circling around the idea of the value we put on human life, and specifically how it relates to our foreign policies, I received an email from my friend Aeon which began with this sentence: 'Human Life is not the Bottom Line in the Decision-Making Process.' This was the idea I was circling. If you look at which issues that define and guide our actions in foreign policy, there is a long list that does not have protection of non-American life near the top. This is a fundamental flaw. There is no asset more valuable than human life; instinctively, when you look at your family, friends, colleagues and community you know this is true. But this self-evident moral truth, 'human life is the bottom line,' which is the bedrock of our shared values, is nowhere reflected in the of our foreign policy nor of most nations around the world.

* * *

While this book tells the hopeful stories of individuals, organizations and governments who rallied on behalf of endangered people and succeeded in protecting them, this is admittedly one of the least effective ways to end genocidal conduct. We cannot look to individuals to be the long-term solution for ending genocide. We need to create a permanent system that will automatically trigger reactions both suitable, and strong enough to end the killing, and defuse potential situations likely to evolve into killing. A complete system must be put in place that is more than an understaffed agency with a noble vision, a vague mandate and little on-the-ground influence. It should be a sound predictor that has United Nations authority to trigger a rapid-deploy force to halt massacres on the ground. In recent years we have seen exactly this kind of *ad hoc* rapid deploy force stop genocide in its tracks. The French forces that went into Eastern DR Congo in the summer of 2003 stopped the massacres in the Ituri province. The Indonesian government sent 4,000 troops to end the massacres on the island of Sulawesi in 2001 and there are several historical examples when force or aforethought instantly ended massacres. The credible threat of force can bring genocide to an end as well as a multitude of other preventative strategies. Few situations will require military intervention. Once an institutionalized military response precedent has been set, perpetrators will be less likely to follow through with genocidal acts. It is the same with any crime. Crime decreases when there are likely immediate consequences for criminals. The majority of situations that have the potential of genocide can be avoided by conflict prevention, economic pressure, diplomacy, political pressure, humanitarian aid and a range of other options that befit each situation. But a permanent and real military option, in the very specific instance of the initiation of genocide, with a standing military, budget and resources, will afford the international community a last resort and will help make other options more palatable for potential perpetrators. It will create a realistic disincentive to kill.

That was, after all, the lesson of Rwanda. No one had a strategic interest in the area which proved to be fatal for over 800,000 Rwandans. Better early warning and a standing rapid-deploy or other intervention mechanism did not (and still does not) exist and could have saved all of those lives. Even without the moral component of the argument, from a cost-benefit analysis, the cost of prevention in this instance would have been a fraction of the cost that was paid in repair, refugee camps, the spread of instability and of course, in lives.

Today, our local interest is not our *only* interest. The world interest is becoming part of our local interest, whether we like it or not, technology is making our world much smaller. Generations before us have responded to the call for action befitting their time. Leadership and morality are inconvenient burdens, but one that when we, as individuals, nations and the world community shirk it invariably leads to the loss of innocent lives and the diminution of our ethical credibility.

CHAPTER TWO: MY PERSONAL ARMENIA.

The Lesson of Musa Dagh.

My Personal Reasons for Writing this Book.

The Evidence: Handwritten Orders for Genocide.

"To serve Armenia is to serve civilization."[1]

Lord Gladstone

The Lesson of Musa Dagh.

[2] Armenians escaping from Musa Dagh on a French freighter 1915.

In the spring of 1915, the first hint of trouble for Armenians in Turkey was when the Young Turk government

---

[1] Joseph Burtt, *The People of Ararat.* (London: Leonard and Virginia Woolf at the Hogarth Press, 1926), 9.

[2] Armeniapedia.org

sent a directive to the local authorities ordering all Armenian communities disarmed. The justification seemed plausible enough; the rifles handed out to communities several years earlier during a time of strife were no longer necessary now that the threat had passed. However, Turkey was entering the First World War and the justification raised some eyebrows. Nonetheless, the vast majority of Armenians obediently complied. For hundreds of years the Armenian population were second class citizens in the class system of the Ottoman Empire. Compliance and accommodation were a way of life since long before Roman times. The Armenian in town of Musa Dagh (Mount Moses), overlooking the Mediterranean coast, did not comply. A disturbing rumor had reached town and the local Armenian leaders chose to keep the weapons and buried the rifles in a church graveyard. A few days later the order was given for all Armenians of Musa Dagh to gather the belongings they could carry in preparation to be moved in a couple of days. The Armenian townspeople were split, some wanted to avoid trouble and decided to leave with the troops when they arrived, but others, the majority, decided to pack as much food, supplies and arms as possible, fortify themselves atop the great hill overlooking the town of Musa Dagh and hide. Almost all those who left peaceably were killed immediately after they were marched out of town, with the women and children being brutalized and raped. The majority who hid on the top of the hill were eventually discovered. When the Turkish troops came to kill them, they fought with surprising ability and vigor and beat back wave after wave of attacks. They used heavy rocks, the advantage of the terrain, rifles and anything they could think of to defend their families. A former soldier was in their midst and supervised their defense. After forty days, when supplies,

31

ammunition and hope were running low, a passing French-flagged ship responded to their distress flag and the Armenians of Musa Dagh escaped to the ship under the cover of darkness. All survived except the soldier Gabriel Bagradian and his son Stephan. The 40 Days of Musa Dagh is not fiction; I have met Musa Dagh Armenians. The lesson of Musa Dagh is instructive; be prepared. When endangered, prepare to defend, flee or perish.

My Personal Reasons for Writing This Book.

I grew up hearing stories of the Armenian genocide. My mother would not talk about it. But my father, who was not Armenian, told me the stories of family who were killed or fled. That was the beginning of my journey to make sense of how a remarkable and peaceful people could be targeted for death. At family events, when I would look at my relatives, or even today as I look at my children, I could not and cannot comprehend why anyone would ever be offended by these beautiful people. There were two genocides of Armenians in 1894 and 1909 prior to the big genocide in 1915, which killed approximately one of every three Armenians. The earlier genocides occurred at the hands of the Ottoman Sultan Abdul Hamid and the 1915 genocide was ordered by the 'Young Turk' government.

The genocide began April 24th, 1915, with the arrest of the leadership of the Armenian community in Constantinople. The Young Turk government began to round up the Armenian intellectuals, leaders and clergy in Constantinople and sent them inland. Less public scrutiny and transparency always offers human nature the opportunity to do evil without consequences. The Turkish military began to go from town to town, ring the town bell, take the men off to do some work unarmed. The men would be massacred outside town and then the troops would return to do whatever they wished to the

women and children. The men and women were so unsuspecting of the troop's motives they went willingly to their own execution. Sometimes, the women and children would be marched into the Deir ez Zor desert and left to starve, which they did. The term 'starving Armenians' became a well-known phrase throughout the world during this crisis.

This was the Twentieth Century's first missed opportunity to develop a legal channel to restrict such activity. Humanity was indeed shocked by what had occurred. Even in the face of staggering First World War casualties, the world community recognized the particularly heinous nature of these massacres. This was wholesale slaughter rarely witnessed since the time of Genghis Khan.

My great-grandfather was killed in front of my great grandmother. He was chopped to pieces by heavy sword. My great grandmother then fled across the Dier ez Zor desert hiding in caves, the same caves that Syrians are hiding in today (2014). In one instance, my great grandmother told my father that when the Turkish troops were so close to a group of twenty hiding Armenians, a young mother held her newborn baby so tightly to muffle its cries, she accidentally smothered it to death.

Great grandma's friend Topal Serpic told how, driven by starvation, she marveled when she saw fruit atop a tree, until she noticed what was underneath it. Many severed head lay scattered around the base of the tree. Unable to climb the tree, with shaking hands, she stacked several of the severed Armenian heads in a staircase of heads that she carefully climbed. She steadied herself and carefully straightened and reached for the fruit. She slipped. The nightmare of being enveloped in a sea of heads was one that reoccurred throughout the rest of her life.

My grandfather, a young shepherd, was adopted by a Turkish family until arrangements could be made for him to immigrate to Canada. Grandma, his future wife, hid in Constantinople in a Muslim School that was a secret Christian abbey by night, until she too could flee to Canada. Eventually, those family members who survived gravitated toward Brantford, Ontario, where my mother was born in 1925. Our family was among the lucky ones, losing only great grandfather and several of his family, but the children survived.

Lord Gladstone spoke to the British Parliament about rescuing the Armenians in their desperate plight at the end of World War Two. He spoke of the need for civilization never to stand by and let that sort of massacre happen again. "To serve the cause of the Armenians is to serve the cause of civilization." It was an idealistic age; few would imagine that a century later civilization would continue to fail in that service of humanity.

The Evidence.

Perpetrators of genocides rarely leave a clear paper trail with descriptions, orders and correspondence as did the 'Young Turk' government did regarding the Armenian genocide. While first-hand reports exist in many languages, the clearest evidence is the documentation of the genocide by the 'Young Turk' leadership, itself. Included here are copies of the actual written orders for genocide signed by Ismail Enver. I found the following documents in the appendices of an Italian book on genocide published in 1962 in a library in Geneva. Having looked at every English and French book in the HEI University library on genocide, I turned to the German and Italian books.

Crouching down to read the titles from the bottom shelf, I noticed a distinctive-looking large old book in Italian. It had the words 'Nella Questione Armena.' Thinking there was only one question that warrants a book regarding Armenians, I flipped through the book scanning to see if anything looked interesting. What I found in the appendices of this book was astonishing.

COLTA DI SCIENZE POLITICHE DELL UNIVERSITÀ DI PADOVA

FRANCESCO SIDARI

LA QUESTIONE ARMENA
NELLA POLITICA DELLE GRANDI POTENZE
dalla chiusura del Congresso di Berlino del 1878
al trattato di Losanna del 1923

PADOVA   CEDAM   1962

There, translated in Italian from the original handwritten Arabic, were what appeared to be documents dating back to the Armenian massacres, with the signatures of Enver Pasha and Talaat Bey, two of the architects of the genocide against the Armenians. I could make out that the letters were about the Armenians. Could it be that I was looking at one of the only surviving copies of the handwritten order for genocide, actually signed by the Young Turk leaders? Four months later, back at Georgetown University, I had my answer. I had stopped by the Italian Department at Georgetown to seek help in translating the documents. A quiet woman, sitting at a desk in the department, agreed to help. Halfway through typing the translation, her fingers halted. She turned slowly to me:

"Do you know what this document is?"

"I am not sure. But I think I do." I said.

"It's" She blinked and looked at it again.

"It's the handwritten order for the extermination of Armenians." She was appalled with disbelief:

"Armenians and those who have an Armenian name…will be killed. Make sure the killings occur with no hesitation or mercy of children of one month of age through all old people ninety years of age does not take place within cities in the view of the population."

On this piece of paper was the handwritten order for the Armenian genocide. This piece of paper led to the deaths of some of my family and one million Armenians. It was very similar to a record I had read about Genghis Khan's orders for the destruction of a race of people who had resisted his forces. 'Let all of their people perish who are taller than an ox cartwheel.' Here was the ancient scourge of humanity in black and white writing, against my family.

Allegato N. 1

STATO MAGGIORE
DELL'OTTAVO CORPO D'ARMATA IMPERIALE

Sezione 2529

Traduzione

MINISTERO   COPIA

2529.

Dal superiore Comando in capo in seconda è stato comunicato che senza ordine del Quartiere Generale non venga trasferito fuori del paese alcun armeno, sia esso uomo o donna e di qualsiasi età.

Inoltre

2597.

1. Tra gli Armeni che dovranno essere trasferiti, le famiglie di coloro che stato sotto la tutela di militari o di impiegati statali rimarranno nei luoghi in cui già risiedevano.

2. Qualora costoro superino nei paesi o villaggi in cui rimangono il numero di cinque case, a partire dalle famiglie di militari, verranno distribuiti in villaggi musulmani di loro scelta, nell'interno dei distretti (kaza) e sangiaccati, da cui dipendono, a patto però di non superare la suddetta densità, e essendo osservata, nei limiti del cento, la proporzione del cinque per cento.

3. In tal modo in un villaggio musulmano di venti case potrà trovar posto non più di solo una casa armena.

4. Nei paesi e villaggi di cento e più case potranno trovar posto non più di cinque case.

5. Disposizioni in questo senso sono state impartite dal Ministero degli Interni al villaggi.

6. Le liste delle famiglie del ribelli verranno compilate al più presto e consegnate ai funzionari locali.

7. Questi ordini del superiore Comando in capo in seconda sono stati riferiti letteralmente.

Se vi sono famiglie di soldati o impiegati che sino a ora sono state trasferite, verrà loro concesso di ritornare.

2 agosto 1331 (2 agosto 1915).

Al Comando Centrale.

Sono state riportate sopra letteralmente le copie di due ordini pervenuti al Comando in seconda della Quarta Armata. Si significa che si procede a norma delle loro disposizioni.

8 agosto 1331 (8 agosto 1915).

Il Vice Comandante dell'Ottavo Corpo d'Armata

One of these documents is here translated.

Attachment
"The same documents of attachment no. 6 and 4.
In addition:

One line in Armenian: The secret of events of March 2, 1918
(Damascus). Telegraph to Damascus.

In Turkish:

Because of the present situation the total extinction of the
Armenian race has been decided (or deliberated) by High Decree.

1. We will act as follows toward the Armenians:
2. The Armenians and those who have an Armenian name
    who are among the inhabitants of the realm protected
    by God with the exception of children up to the age of
    five years of age will be killed, being the rebels who
    were taken out of towns and villages.
3. All the Armenian military who are currently employed
    in the Imperial Army will be separated from their units
    without provoking incidents and killed by gun in a
    concealed place without contact with the local
    population.
4. The Armenian officers that are in the army will be
    imprisoned in the general quarters of the units to
    which they belong until a new order is issued.
5. Since specific letters will circulate regarding the
    execution of these three articles after 48 hours since

---

[3] La Questione Armena Nella Politica delle Grandi Potenze by F. Sidari.
Padova: Scienze Polotiche dell'Universita, 1962. Appendix.

the date of their (the letters) arrival at the headquarters of each unit, no action is to be taken before except for necessary preparations.

Second in Command

Enver

The same document as attached no. 2.

In addition:

Copy of the telegram send by Talaat Pasha to Atif Bey, 'Vali' of Ankara:

Make Sure the killings with no hesitation and mercy of children one month of age through all old people of 90 years of age does not take place within cities in the presence (view) of the population."[4]

As someone who has grown up hearing accounts from family and has spent a portion of my adult life researching the Armenian genocide, I see no room for doubt of the veracity of the genocide. The signed orders, the first-hand accounts, in several languages, by hundreds of witnesses, and hundreds and hundreds of thousands of survivors leads me to believe that any objective scholar would confirm credibility of what common sense and evidence has clearly demonstrated. This unfortunate denial was and still is the accepted policy of the Turkish government. Though no perpetrators are alive today, and the Turkish government today bears little resemblance to the 'Young Turk' government a century ago, its continued denial

---

[4] Ibid., Appendix.

of the obvious, is more than hurtful, it makes modern Turkey subtly complicit with the actions of a previous government it would otherwise have little in common. Only in recent years have the first publications in Turkish appeared to begin to discuss the Armenian genocide in public. It is a matter of respect for the dead, setting the record straight and acknowledging the preciousness of the lives lost.

Far from distancing themselves from the genocide, the ruling 'Young Turk' troika confirmed that they were responsible for the Armenian Genocide in a conversation with the U.S Ambassador Morganthau to Turkey. Enver Pasha and Talaat Bey's assured the US Ambassador and German Embassy officials in Turkey that they were directly responsible for the killing.

In reply to the US Ambassador Morgenthau who was deploring the massacres against the Armenian and attributing them to irresponsible underlings in the distant provinces, Enver's reply was:

> "You are greatly mistaken. We have this country absolutely under our control. I have no desire to shift blame onto our underlings and I am entirely willing to accept the responsibility myself for everything that has taken place."

In a conversation with Mordtmann of the German Embassy in June of 1915 Talaat said:

> "Turkey is taking advantage of the war in order to thoroughly liquidate internal foes, (i.e. the indigenous Christians), without thereby being disturbed by foreign intervention."

After the German Ambassador persistently brought up the Armenian question in 1918, Talaat said with a smile:
"What on earth do you want? The question is settled. There are no more Armenians."[5]

There was no shame on the part of the perpetrators. They justified the horror that had occurred throughout Turkey as a useful tool to solidify their nation and religion.

As with all known genocides, Turkey had bystanders who were indifferent, or took part in the criminal activity or heroic. A number of Turkish individuals and families helped hide, smuggle and even adopt some of their Armenian neighbor's children. Many survivors' accounts bear witness to this credit to human nature. Some took orphaned Armenian children into their homes. Others nourished fleeing Armenians and helped them on their way. But large portions of the Turkish population were presented with a *fait accompli*. One day they had Armenian neighbors and the next day they were gone; they were being marched out of town with some of their belongings. While some Turkish or Kurdish neighbors benefited from the abandoned Armenian homes and belongings, others sought to help their neighbors and friends.

The secrecy of the plan was essential, otherwise the remaining Armenian population would have panicked at the oncoming massacres and armed themselves. This secrecy was crucial during the Holocaust as well. In the towns of Sivas, Van and others, resistance was organized to no avail, except for Musa Dagh, where most of the population escaped to a French

---

[5] Vahakn, Dadrian, *Genocide: A Critical Bibliographical Review* http://www.cilicia.com/armo10a.html

41

freight ship through a combination of tenacity, foresight and incredible luck.[6] Musa Dagh had an escape route that other Armenian cities and neighborhoods did not.

Far from being indifferent to the plight of the Armenians, the Allied European powers and some of Turkey's German allies, denounced the Turkish genocidal activities. The world was shocked and began clamoring for something to be done about it. What exactly could be done about it was difficult to envision until the Ottoman/Turkish forces were defeated. The time for preventative action had passed years before.

Once the massacres had ended, the allies and international organizations sent aid to the Armenians. The issue of how this utterly devastated nation could be protected so it could rebuild was thoroughly discussed. The ideas ranged from the concept of a French protectorate, to an American protectorate, to the independence of traditional Armenia as outlined in the Treaty of Sevres. No action to protect the Armenians occurred, however, because within a short period of time the re-formed Turkish forces swept the allies and the new fledgling independent Armenian state from Anatolia. The Allies, weary of war, relented to the domestic opposition to prolonged foreign entanglement and ultimately the *de facto* ground situation became permanent. The issue of independence for Armenia was dropped shortly after a joint Turkish-Soviet invasion partitioned the nation in 1921.

There were no trials of the people responsible for the genocide. Herein lies the final enduring lessons of the Armenian tragedy. There was no punishment for the

---

[6] Franz Werfel, *The Forty Days of Musa Dagh.* (New York: Carol and Graf Publishing, 1991).

perpetrators, no apology or acknowledgement by the new Turkish government for the actions of the 'Young Turk' government. The apology or acknowledgement is an important step in the victim community's ability to heal and move on from genocide. The lack of accountability and acknowledgement may be part of the reason why a sense of despair and mourning was reflected in ethos of many of the older Armenians who seemed to permanently wear black as if reflexive of that state of mourning. More importantly for the world, no protections were created to safeguard against similar activity in the future.

The Armenian genocide became the blueprint for many genocides to come, with the key steps being:

- Vilify and disarm the minority
- Remove them to remote locations and as quickly and secretly as possible
- Kill them.

Without early warning and response capacity to anticipate and defuse future genocide and massacres, mankind was, and remains, destined to repeat itself.

In Turkey today, it is only beginning to be possible to talk about the Armenian Genocide, but it is still quite dangerous and controversial to do so. The only thing that ties the present government to the 'Young Turks', ironically, is their denial of the 'Young Turk' acts – their continuation of this denial is what makes them subtly complicit. In a letter in August 2013 to the Washington Post, the Turkish Foreign Minister rightly decried the genocide occurring in Syria. It has occurred near Homs, in the countryside, in cities and in the Deir ez Zor desert. The Deir ez Zor, the same desert to which my great-grandmother fled, where her friend Topal Serpic climbed a mountain of severed heads, where a generation of Armenian women and children were left without food and water to die. The desert has remained the same, and so has the crime.

CHAPTER THREE: 20TH CENTURY GENOCIDE.

UKRAINE HOLODOMOR (1932-1933).

"On the battlefield men die quickly, they fight back, they are sustained by fellowship and a sense of duty. Here I saw people dying in solitude by slow degrees."

> - Victor Kravchenko, a former communist activist on the Ukraine starvation of the Holodomor.

The use of starvation as a tactic to depopulate an area would not end with my ancestors the Armenians. In less than fifteen years, between five to ten million Ukrainian farmers would be intentionally starved to death. The perpetrator was Soviet leader Joseph Stalin and his policies designed to end a nascent independence movement and force the collectivization of farms.

Ethnic and religious massacre and genocide had existed for millenniums. The targeting of a specific nationality is only a few hundred years old because of the newness of the modern phenomenon of the nation-state. But ideological genocide and ideological mass atrocities are phenomenon borne of the 20th Century.

In 1932, Joseph Stalin was ending his first brutal, but successful, five-year plan. His massive program of rapid industrialization was fortified with a ruthlessness that the Czars had rarely approached. Calling in sick and arriving late to work were often considered indications of counter revolutionary thought and were punishable by exile to Siberian work camps. While iron ore and steel production had doubled in four years, the collectivization of privately-owned farms was slower to take shape. Stalin had decided to double his industrial efforts and attempt to finish the collectivization of all privately-owned farms in his second five-year plan. Old opposition forces began to take root in Ukraine where the kulak farmers sought to protect their farms and way of life. This resistance to collectivism and the independence movement were cause for immediate concern to the acutely paranoid Stalin.

The last civil war between 'red' and 'white' Russians was still a recent memory and the thought of starting another civil war, on national fault lines as well as ideological ones, did not appeal to Stalin. Instead, he sent Soviet soldiers into Ukraine - not to invade, but to seize all grain, harvests and livestock from the farms throughout this fertile region. Then a nation starved to death. The most conservative estimates place the number of Ukrainians who perished at between 5-6 million. Stalin himself and others close to the Soviet leadership estimated the number to be ten million killed. Entire villages starved out of existence. Entire regions were devastated as if by a bomb that left the landscape devoid of most human life but the buildings still standing.

This strategy was not new. From ancient times through the Middle Ages, armies sieged and starved towns and kingdoms into submission. It was only fifty-five years before the Holodomor (Ukraine starvation) that United States President Rutherford B. Hayes used starvation as a weapon against the Sioux Confederacy in 1877. Hayes could not envision remobilizing the Union forces when the nation was trying to put the bloodshed of the civil war behind it. An inexpensive and simple solution was to send soldiers and contractors into the American plains to annihilate the Buffalo. Without their dietary staple of Buffalo, the Sioux Confederation tribes starved. Some migrated to Canada, and others surrendered to be confined to reservations.

The use of starvation as a tool of war has been repeated since the Sioux, the Armenians, and the Ukrainians, throughout the Twentieth Century to include the Ibo of Nigeria, and in more history the non-Party members in North Korea and Zimbabwe, the Nuba of Sudan, and recently in al Shabaab-controlled areas of Somalia. Starvation has been used as a military or political tool and a method of genocide in each decade of the past one hundred years. Famine when used by regimes and militias as a tool of warfare against civilians renders the perpetrators as guilty of genocide as those perpetrated it with gas, machetes or guns.

Though the UN Genocide Convention definition of genocide does not specifically include ideological groups as potential victims, the Ukrainian Famine of 1932-33 was indisputably genocide. It was orchestrated against the Ukrainian nationalist movement and directed by Stalin. Crops seized from the farmers were used for internal Soviet redistribution and for sale outside of the Soviet Union. Storage granaries in Ukraine were emptied and millions of Ukrainians perished.

Ukrainians fled the famine when they could. Many attempted to flee to the Caucuses but were usually caught and returned to Ukraine to starve. Soon the railroads and other transportation authorities made escape almost impossible

"...in connection with mass exodus of peasants beyond the borders of Ukraine... the Commissar of Railways and...transport divisions to immediately inform all railway stations about the suspension of ticket sales for destinations beyond Ukraine's borders to villagers who have not secured permission to leave from their (district)."[7]

The children were perhaps the greatest victims of all. They easily succumbed to illnesses and starvation. Royal Consul Gradenigo of Italy described the horror that awaited children and adults who became too weak or ill.

"A week ago a special service was created to catch unsupervised children. There are also children brought here and left by parents who went back to their villages to die. They hope that someone in the city will provide shelter and take care of them. Lately, these children could be seen crawling and crying on the sidewalks. One newborn was sucking milk from the breast of its gray-faced, dead mother.

The swollen are shuttled on freight trains to rural areas 50 to 60 kilometers outside the city where nobody can see them die. The railcars are filled up and bolted shut. I learned these details from the health workers and can

---

[7] Resolution of the CC CPU Politburo executing January 22 Order from USSR SNK and CC AUCP(b). January 23, 1933. Pp. 86-87.

thus guarantee the reliability of this information."[8]
Report from the Consul of Italy.

These scenes rival the gruesomeness of any genocides –
the horrible fate of millions of children and the lack of human
dignity shown to hundreds of thousands of victims in various
acts of defilement, are among the basest activities in human
experience. The diplomat concluded with his belief that the
Ukraine would be 'Russified' and lose its Ukrainian
character.[9]" How prescient; this is certainly proving to be
true in the South and East Ukraine and has contributed to
instability in the early years of modern Ukraine's fledgling
democracy.

---

[8] Report from the Consul of Italy in Kharkiv to the Minister of Foreign
Affairs of Italy on "Famine and the Ukrainian Situation." May 31, 1933.
Pp. 107 – 109.

[9] Ibid.

The Soviet Union Purges (1934 – 1939).

> "How can I know you so long after sad separation, Where's your voice, glance, and face upon which I so strongly depend? Where's the dear hand that touched me with caring and loving sensation? Tell me, how can I know you so long after sad separation, after tears without end."

Maria Taurke

Poem to her husband who never returned.

In the 1930s, the world witnessed some of the worst ideologically based mass atrocities at the hands of the Soviet Union's dictator Joseph Stalin. He victimized his own people in the Soviet Union in the name of counter revolutionary purges. The 'great purge' destroyed lives, families and communities and left scars that are still felt today. Some scholars do not include 'ideologically-based' massacres as genocide – I do. My friend, Sasha, has a powerful presence and is a decorated American Colonel. Sasha's father was dragged away in the middle of the night and executed for a crime that didn't exist.

"Father's Arrest in the Middle of the Night.

By Erwin Alexander ("Sasha") Taurke

For ten years, Mother and Father had consciously decided not to have children. Conditions just were not right – too much hunger, too much insecurity, too many purges – who in their right minds would want to bring children into this kind of world? Finally, in the early nineteen thirties, it seemed to

Mother and Father that the cycle was broken. The terror had receded. The population was urged to live without fear and produce again. And Mother and Father decided to try for a child, and on the fourth of May 1934, the overjoyed couple received a baby boy.

The photo album shows typical family bliss: the boy at one month; the boy at a month and a half, the boy at two months; the boy at three and at six months, and a year, and a year and a half, and two. The boy is being carried proudly by Father on shoulders, is shown in Mother's arms, is lying naked on the beach, is with relatives on an outing; the boy at two and a half. Then the photographs stop for a long period of time, and when they appear again, the father is no longer there.

Father was arrested in the early fall of 1937 in the typical fashion - at night past the midnight hours, with a loud, peremptory banging on the door and a shouting "open immediately or the door goes." Frightened but curious corridor neighbors (who are also curiously thankful that it isn't them) peek out of their doors in blankets and nightclothes. A squad of huge, booted men marches in. While the leader barks: "You are under arrest, get dressed and come with us," the others begin to ransack the room, searching for whatever incriminating evidence they can find, or manufacture. The frightened family is only given minutes to say good-bye to each other before the arrested member is marched off.

Father leaned over my little bed. Half-wakened by the noise, I stirred and then, through my sleep, recited my favorite poem, from my most favorite bedtime book about a little engine that could, and traveling far away but coming back:

> Firemen are at the engine;
> Steam is rising from the engine.
> Fare you well! We're on our way.
> We'll be back some other day.

At any rate, that's what I remember vaguely from my childhood, because I stopped liking the story.

Tears falling on my cover do not help. Father is led away. This is the last time that my mother sees my father ever again.

Father had several sessions with his interrogator throughout the last weeks of his freedom. He would come home, shaken and pale, crawl under the blankets, and whisper to Mother what he had endured. Of course he was not supposed to talk, since he was sworn to secrecy after each interrogation session. Mother said that Father was asked several times to betray someone else and to become a secret collaborator, but he refused. Perhaps this was the ultimate reason for his final arrest and his subsequent fate.

Once a person is in the clutches of the secret police system, he disappears as if into a black hole. All contact with him is refused. No news of his condition is ever given. No reason for an arrest is offered. Desperate family members go to the secret police office, only to be told, again and again, to come back later. And you are spoken to only if there is an offering presented to the official. With mother, this lasted for about six months. Finally, in the middle of winter, she got word that my father, in accordance with Article 58 of the criminal code, was sentenced to 10 years of hard labor "under conditions of severe isolation."

"Severe isolation" meant that for the duration of the sentence there would be no news of the prisoner. No letters are allowed. No packages can be sent. No visits are possible. The person may die, and their loved one may not know for years what happened. It's just yet another nice twist of totalitarian justice. However, even in the harshest totalitarian system, there are always ways to find out what happened, despite the best efforts of the regime. Shortly after getting the official information about him, Mother received a so-called blood notice that Father was shot. Blood notices are little pieces of clothing, sometimes a flat stone, sometimes a piece of wood, upon which, scratched by a nail or written in blood, is a short message about a prisoner. When prisoners are sentenced to hard labor, they are transported to their assigned labor camps under guard in cattle cars with barbed wire on openings. After writing the message on a torn bit of his clothing, or some other material, the prisoner then pushes the message out of the boxcar through cracks in the slats onto the tracks. After the train leaves, villagers from around the area gather and check the tracks for messages, and then try to get the messages to relatives, because they hope that they themselves will get messages about their own loved ones when and if their time comes.

The message read: "Karl Taurke. Kiev. Shot"

Immediately after my father was sentenced, Mother was declared to be the "wife of the enemy of the people" and issued a so-called "Wolf's Pass." Under a "Wolf Pass," the person has to report every week to a police station to obtain a stamp that one has done so. The neat twist is that the person cannot report to any police station twice, and thus is forced to go all over town to find a police station to report to that is different from all the previous ones. A "Wolf's Pass" therefore is usually a pass to certain dislocation and often to starvation.

As it was, terrible indeed must have been the time when my mother finally had to stand on the platform waiting for a train out of Kiev, marked as a wife of an enemy of the people and looking at an uncertain future, holding my hand in the bitter cold, while her son, orphaned by the regime, shivered and blue with cold, yet intoned: "I am not c-c-cold, mamma, because I am a hero of Soviet Stalin." Thus a truly totalitarian regime pushes children into partaking of its crimes.

Mother was truly devastated by the loss of her husband and never really got over it. When the mood struck her, she provided a counterpoint to the happy stories about Father and her, saying that in her entire life she experienced only thirteen happy years, the years she spent with Father. When she died at the age of 93 in 1996, I went through her things. Because Alzheimer's disease struck her in her last years, resulting in severe paranoia, she had destroyed most of her photographs, but I found an album and took her favorite picture of my father off the wall of her house. The frame was not in very good shape, and I left the frame, placing the photograph in the album. Only later did I happen to be looking through the album and found faint letters on the back of Father's photo. It was a poem, written by Mother, who was not a bad poet at all. It goes like this:

How can I know you so long after sad separation?
Where's your voice, glance, and face upon which I so
strongly depend?

Where's the dear hand that touched me with caring and
loving sensation?

Tell me, how can I know you so long after sad separation,
after tears without end.

It was so long ago, I don't even remember it clearly,

But the nights without sleep, and the thoughts, and the fears
torture me!

How I wish to be joyful! How memories rise up so dearly!

It was so long ago, I don't even remember you clearly,

But you're always with me!

I must be frank with you; I cannot read this poem without tears."

The fate of Sasha's father is similar to millions of other non-offending and innocent people caught in purges that placated a paranoid leader. These lives fed the insatiable appetite for new victims of a state killing machine Stalin created. Now a grandfather, Sasha, can still feel the kiss that his father laid upon his head as he bid farewell and promised to return soon.

The particular purge that killed Sasha's father was the great terror of 1936. Officially, it lasted from 1934 – 1939. Stalin began the terror by giving the order to kill Kirov a rising star in the Soviet leadership. Stalin blamed the assassination on counterrevolutionaries used this as an excuse to begin the purge. Any perceived enemies of Stalin's, old party leaders, influential officers, former landowners, German speakers were targets. A quota existed in each district of how many victims needed to be executed each month, regardless of guilt, and the quota was always filled. Overall, Stalin's great terror of 1936 killed: 2 million civilians, 30,000 officers, the entire politburo, 80% of generals and 90% of colonels. [10]

[10] *Communist Nations Since 1917*. Ch. 3: Russia under Lenin and Stalin, Anna Cienciala, Kansas University, 2010.
http://acienciala.faculty.ku.edu/communistnationssince1917/ch3.html

THE HOLOCAUST (1934 – 1945).

The Charlene Schiff Story.
Individual and Governmental Heroism and Evil.
Pastor Trocme – Simple Resistance.
Un-Police Like Duty.
The Wallenberg-Eichmann Debate.
The 'Europa Plan.'
Bulgaria – Defying Hitler.
Denmark – Widespread Rescue of Jews.
The Wannsee Conference.

"The world is too dangerous a place to live in – not because of the people who do evil, but because of the people who stand by and let them."

Albert Einstein

In the early weeks of the CPG's founding, the Board of Directors invited two speakers who had survived genocide to come speak to us; Charlene Schiff was the first.

The Charlene Schiff Story.

The door to the office opened and a small elderly lady resembling Doctor Ruth Westheimer entered smiling into the board of directors' meeting. I introduced Charlene Schiff to the C.P.G board. We had to place a small platform behind the podium so she could stand and see over it.

She thanked us for the invitation to the C.P.G and began to tell her story. She told how her family had lived in Poland and were forced into the Jewish ghetto at the beginning of the war, and how difficult life was in the ghetto. She said it was made bearable because her mother and family were there. One day her mother had found a hole in the wall that led to outside the ghetto. It was just barely large enough for each of them to squeeze through and her mother told her that if trouble began, they would flee through the hole.

Months later when the shots rang out and the screams could be heard, they knew that the ghetto was being liquidated. They ran quickly to the wall in darkness, found the hole and crawled through it. They ran to a wooded area where they hid for the rest of the night. By morning the shots had stopped, and Charlene's mother told her that she would go back quickly to see if any of their family had survived in any of the hiding places. Charlene begged her mother not to go. It was the last time she would see her.

At this point, Charlene stopped speaking to gather herself together. The pain of losing her mother and the thought that she should have begged her to wait longer was always with her. Could she have stopped her from going back? Charlene waited for her mother until late that evening when hunger drove her toward the outskirts of town where she rummaged through trash to find food. For months she lived by scavenging out of garbage and hiding from all human contact. One day she came across a group of twelve other children who were also from the ghetto who had banded together and were surviving much the same way she was. She joined them. She made friends and they bonded together in their common fears and needs. They talked and played and shared the dangers of their existence and the

58

memories of their families. These were the kinds of friends you would keep for life. For twelve of them this was to be true.

One morning as they were gathering food from garbage cans near the outskirts of a town, some town children saw them. There was a moment when neither side moved. Then the town children ran shrieking back to alert the town of the Jewish children's presence. The townspeople roused themselves and headed out to the fields with pitchforks. Charlene and her friends climbed into large rolls of hay. They could just squeeze themselves into the stacks and not be seen from the outside. Yet the villagers found them. They surrounded the big rolls of hay and methodically stabbed the haystack with their pitchforks until the children screamed and their blood flowed. By the end of the morning all twelve of the children were dead, except Charlene.

She dabbed her eyes, and the board room was still. Hers was the story of genocide. Everyone in the room at the Center for the Prevention of Genocide was affected. They now felt genocide.

After she spoke each of the board members approached her and shook her hand and spoke with her for a while. We took a brief break. Then she joined the board at the table.

"Who, after all, speaks today of the annihilation of the Armenians?"[11]

Adolf Hitler

Individual and Governmental Heroism and Evil.

The Holocaust was not a monolithic undertaking by the Third Reich alone. Its success was aided by the collaboration of Nazi allies, the conquered, the disinterested and a lawless international superstructure which was unable or unwilling to block a well-organized genocide. The consequences of the failure to create binding International laws after the Armenian genocide, laws with effective sanctions and mechanisms to prevent genocide, were felt throughout Europe only twenty years later, and throughout the world for the next century.

As incredible as it may seem, some of the Holocaust could have been prevented or curtailed. This goes beyond the scope of theoretical International law, early warning and possible sanctions created at the end of World War One. There existed several means that could have significantly altered the Nazi policy of extermination. For example, there were negotiations to ransom and rescue the Jews across Europe, the 'Europa Plan,' which was tested successfully. There was the military option of bombing the train tracks that led to the Concentration Camps. There was effective action, sabotage and disobedience in governments conquered by and allied with the Third Reich. We will look at some of those governments' responses. In this chapter we will look at three examples of

---

[11] Vahakn Dadrian, *Genocide, A Critical Biographical Review.*
http://cilicia.com/armo10a.html

heroic reactions from individuals to help save lives during the Holocaust. These heroes range from the wealthy diplomat Raoul Wallenberg, who quietly saved tens of thousands of Jews through creative endeavors, paying for it with his freedom. They include a Pastor whose refusal to salute the fascist flag at his school was the first act of defiance that led to a town's almost universal complicity in hiding and saving Jewish children.

These heroes are not, however, the answer for genocide prevention. It is the lesson of this book that the unavoidable answer to genocide is the creation of an early warning system that can trigger a rapid response from the international community including a possible rapid deployment of a standing armed force. A standing UN force should be dedicated to responding to genocide, mass atrocities and the threat of either and be capable of intervening in areas where there is no political interest or will to protect civilians being massacred. A far less effective remedy to genocide is through the action of people who are in a position to help - the ministers and generals, the leaders and administrators who can alter, end or sabotage the process of death. These individuals, in our case, include a diplomat, a pastor and an industrialist.

While not the permanent answer, the following examples provide courageous blueprints for action under the worst duress. Their actions ran counter to the national indifference engulfing their nations. These three examples can give us hope that with clear-headed moral certitude, individuals, even flawed ones, can save thousands of lives. During the Holocaust, many people remained indifferent due to disbelief, callousness, self-preservation, national association and helplessness, among many reasons.

61

Pastor Trocme – Simple Resistance.

One of the most notable resistances to the policy of deportation and extermination came from a small community named Le Chambon in southeastern France. The people of Le Chambon were a community engaged in the rare fight against persecution in the name of their religious ideals, for the sake of humanity. Some resisted the authorities openly, placing themselves in great personal jeopardy. In an historic account of the actions of Pastor Trocme, his colleagues and the entire town, Philip Hallie's *Lest innocent Blood Be Shed* gives us an account that should be a blueprint for future genocidal resistance by third parties.

Resistance to human rights and genocidal abuse must begin somewhere and can start with simple action. The Vichy government had required that all schools begin their day with a morning salute to the fascist flag. Most members of the faculty went through the daily ritual and thus began their complicity by dull acceptance.

The distinction between the passive collaboration and those who resisted could hinge on a given decision on a given day. But what action or incident can begin to jar the indifferent out of their torpor? At a certain point average men and women who realize the impetus to act, often internalize their commitment to help their fellow man without a word being said. What brings an individual to a point where they must face themselves to assess their morals and the value of their action or inaction? Once a person comes to that turn in the road the road there is no turning back. Even if one were to stop helping, one still knows what should be done. This was the will that flourished in this small town. Throughout Europe, heroism, criminality and indifference occurred often on the same street. In one town, most made the commitment to help.

One morning, at the local school where Pastor Andre Trocme taught, when the fascist Vichy flag was raised, the entire faculty and staff saluted or half saluted it with the notable exception of Pastor Trocme.

> "The government was not aware of what happened (not saluting the flag) at Le Chambon. But the three thousand people of Le Chambon were fully aware. Moreover, they saw that they could resist, that there was a possibility of resisting. For them it was like having a new, beautifully colored bird pointed out, a bird they had never seen before. But now that they saw it...they knew it could come back."[12]

Shortly after Pastor Trocme silently refused to salute the Vichy flag, the trickle of Jewish orphans began to arrive in Le Chambon where they found refuge at the Pastor's home. When the number became unmanageable, he asked parishioners of his church to house some of the orphans; and they agreed. When the number became too great for the congregation, the townspeople were prevailed upon. It was not long before most of Le Chambon was complicit in this openly kept secret mission.

The timing of his simple act of resistance, not saluting the Nazi flag, which led to other activities and inspired his town,

---

[12] Philip Haile, *Lest Innocent Blood Be Shed.*, 91.

could not have been more important. It provides an example of hope that simple resistance can lead to preventing genocide.

When a high-ranked official of the Vichy government visited Le Chambon, the community's resistance was not discussed until a young man approached the minister and delivered the following letter. The unequivocal tenor of the message could have led to the young man's instant death; instead it may have led to the reconsideration of a political crackdown in the area.

"Mr. Minister:

We have learned of the frightening scenes which took place three weeks ago in Paris, where the French police, on orders from the occupying power, arrested in their homes all of the Jewish families in Paris to hold them in the Vel d'Hiv. The fathers were torn from their families and sent to Germany. The children were torn from their mothers, who underwent the same fate as their husbands. Knowing by experience that the decrees of the occupying power are, with brief delay, imposed upon unoccupied France, where they are presented as spontaneous decisions of the head of the French government, we are afraid that the measures of deportation of the Jews will soon be applied to the Southern Zone.

We feel obligated to tell you that there are among us a certain number of Jews. But we make no distinction between Jews and non-Jews. It is contrary to the Gospel teaching.

Of our comrades, whose only fault is to be born of another religion, receive the order to let themselves be deported, or even examined, they would disobey the orders received, and we would try to hide them as best we could." [13]

This firm conviction expressed by the young man and the townspeople surprised the Vichy officials who did not quite know how to react. Later, when the Gestapo freely operated in the South, there would be a telephone call warning of an imminent raid on Chambon warning before one would occur. [14] This implies that this act was one of the Vichy policemen, who had been stationed in Le Chambon. It shows us that courageous defiance can become infectious.

Un-Police-Like Duty.

The people of Le Chambon distinguished themselves in their service to protect Jewish orphans during the Holocaust. But many communities and many average people throughout Europe, would surprisingly participate in the criminal treatment of the Jews. One would expect average fathers and grandfathers to take exception to the policy of extermination and certainly one would not expect them *not* to actively take part in the killing if asked. Christopher Browning's account of average older men doing this unthinkable thing is riveting and a terrible example

---

[13] Ibid., 102-105
[14] Ibid., 114.

of the content of character of some average people when prevailed upon to kill.

Browning's Account of 'Ordinary Men' Committing Genocide

"In the early morning of July 13th, 1942, the men of the Reserve Police Battalion 101 were roused from their bunks. They were middle-aged family men of working and lower middle class background from the City of Hamburg. Considered to be too old to be of use to the German Army, they had been drafted Into the Order Police. Most were raw recruits with no previous experience.. It was still quite dark as the men climbed into the waiting trucks. They were headed toward their first major action, though the men had not yet been told what to expect. (The Convoy arrived in Jozefow and the men climb out of the truck to be addressed by their commander).

Pale and nervous. With choking voice and tears in his eyes, (Papa) Trapp fought to control himself as he spoke. The battalion, he said plaintively, had to perform a frightfully unpleasant task. The assignment was not to his liking, indeed it was highly regrettable, but the orders came from the highest authorities. If it would make their task any easier, the men should remember that in Germany the bombs were falling on women and children.

He then turned to the matter at hand. The Jews had instigated the American boycott that had damaged Germany. There were Jews in Jozefow who were involved with the partisans. The battalion had been ordered to round up these Jews. The male Jews of working age were to be separated and taken to a work camp. The remaining Jews – the women, the children and the elderly – were to be shot on the spot by the battalion. Having explained what awaited the men, Trapp then made an extraordinary offer: if any of the older men among them did not feel up to the task that lay ahead, he should step out.

When Trapp first made his offer early in the morning, the real nature of the action had just been announced and time to think and react had been very short. Only a dozen men instinctively seized the moment to step out, turn in their rifles, and thus excuse themselves from the subsequent killings.

Later during the killing one policeman approached his superior and asked for a different assignment and was given one. Soon another group approached the same Sergeant and asked to be excused from the killing and were given another assignment. Another couple of policemen simply milled around and did not participate to the ire of their colleagues and received no disciplinary action. After the firing squad had finished executing the women and children and during the weeks after the "action" there was not one person in the battalion who did not resent what they had been asked to do....a lieutenant Buchmann, asked to be transferred back to Hamburg. He would not take part in Jewish actions because he was not "suited to certain tasks alien to the police." He was transferred without too much trouble. Only 10-20 percent of the battalion did not take part in the killing, the explanation: wartime brutalization, racism, segmentation and routinization of the task, careerism, obedience to orders, deference to authority, conformity."[15]

Here is the answer to the question, 'what would ordinary, average men do, when confronted with being forced to commit genocide?' Most do. During the four years teaching International Human Rights and Conflict in the Modern World, this quotation caused a great amount of ethical dilemma for my students. What is the correct course of action? A couple brutally honest men disclosed that they hated to think they would do it but didn't see a way out of the situation the above quote described. They wouldn't jeopardize their own family's safety. Most students in my classes indicated they would mill around or un-volunteer like some of the police officers chose to do. The bravest held that they would fiercely argue the 'un-police-like duty' nature of the assignment and verbally resist the order until they held sway over Trapp and his men. One boldly claimed he would turn his attention to Trapp and try to free, or warn, the Jews. As much as we would like to assume we would act heroically, most of us would not. Home, family, safety make cowards of many of us. The impossibility of situations like this makes the creation of early warning and detection more crucial. During and after World War Two a popular refrain was 'we should have stopped Hitler at Munich.' Indeed. We should be stopping all future Hitlers, now.

---

[15] Christopher Browning, "Ordinary Men." In *The Holocaust* (New York: Houghton, Mifflin, Co., 1997), 168-171.

The Wallenberg – Eichmann Debate.

Raoul Wallenburg left the safety of Sweden to save more than 100,000 Jewish lives in Budapest, Hungary.

"(Nazism) It's not really a bona fide ideology. *It's just the political incarnation of a single basic human emotion. Hate.* How can it last?" [16]

Raoul Wallenberg,
Heroic Swedish
Diplomat while arguing
with Adolf Eichmann.

---

[16] Danny Smith, *Wallenburg.*1986.

The greatest hero of the Holocaust's name often goes unrecognized by many people today. Raoul Wallenberg is reputed to have saved nearly 100,000 Jewish lives in and around Budapest in the closing months of World War Two. His life and story are astounding and a testimony to the good that can be embodied by the human spirit. As incredible as his life-saving exploits were, the fact that he openly opposed the Holocaust's architect Adolph Eichmann and not only knew him but had dined together and fiercely debated the Nazi doctrine and the Holocaust. This stands as one of the clearest moral debates between good and evil in modern history.

"Budapest, December 1944.

"At the end of private dinner, the small group of men retired to another room for after dinner drinks. The dinner was thrown together quickly by Lars Berg for his colleague, the wealthy Swedish diplomat Raoul Wallenberg. Among the guests was Adolf Eichmann, the Nazi SS officer responsible for the 'final solution' - the murder of all Jews in Third Reich and Axis territory. To this day, Eichmann remains one of the most notorious agents for death and evil in the Twentieth Century. A slight man, Eichmann's mission in Budapest was to finish the deportation of the last 250,000 Hungarian Jews to their death. 400,000 Jews had already been deported under the fascist Hungarian government. Even as the Soviet troops advanced toward Budapest, Eichmann was sent to finish this evil work before Budapest changed hands. By contrast, Raoul Wallenberg's presence in Budapest was as an agent of life, relentlessly pursuing strategies to save as many Jews as possible from the killing machine of the Nazis. He had no delusion about the fate of the Jews being deported, having read the secret reports written by Jews who had escaped Auschwitz. In 1942 after watching a film telling the story of a man saved Jews from German Concentration Camps, He turned to his half-sister Nina and said, 'that's what I want to do.' Two years later he arrived in Budapest as a diplomatic attaché whose mission was to aid endangered Jews." [17]

As soon as Wallenberg arrived to work in the Swedish Legation in Budapest, he used his wealth and untiring energy to create the 'schutzpass' for Jews, a safe-conduct pass for travelers waiting to go to Sweden after the war. This passport was essentially a ruse and had no legal standing except for that which he forced on Hungarian officials. Nonetheless, it provided protection from deportation and death for thousands of Jewish 'schutzpass' holders. Wallenberg paid for a publicity campaign for the official-looking safe-conduct pass with large billboards announcing them throughout Budapest. Before long, Wallenberg was able to obtain large quotas from the fascist government to allow thousands of Jews protection under this passport. He argued, bribed, and threatened a diplomatic incident if the 'schutzpass' was not recognized. When the 'schutzpass' reached its quota limit, he developed another strategy. Leasing entire apartment complexes, Wallenberg claimed them as Swedish diplomatic territory and safely housed hundreds of Jewish families in them. Other neutral countries

---

[17] Ibid.

and humanitarian organizations followed his lead and the number of Jews who were protected in the International ghetto grew. When necessary, Wallenberg would pressure officials with the skill of a lawyer, often forming complex but compelling reasons why the official should give him what he wanted. He even forced a friend to pressure her husband, the Interior Minister of the Arrow Cross fascist government, to reinstate the 'Schutzpass' when it was cancelled. Wallenberg was unstoppable. There are many accounts of Raoul rushing to the river side or to a remote farm where Jews were being lined up to be shot or marched to the death trains. He would go among their number, obtaining names and vital information and issue them protective visas, saving their lives on the spot.

On the last night of the vicious Arrow Cross government, as Budapest was about to fall to the advancing Soviets, the order came to the SS to liquidate the Jewish ghetto of its 60,000 inhabitants. Wallenberg sent a personal note to the SS commander in charge of executing the order. In the note Raoul promised to testify at the officer's trial for crimes against humanity if he gave the order to liquidate the Jewish ghetto. It is likely that Wallenberg's intervention saved those 60,000 lives that night. [18]

> "Eichmann was the guest at Wallenberg's home with excellent food for dinner in Budapest during the last days of the Second World War. After dinner they retired to a room with a view of the Russian artillery shelling in the distance and had after-dinner drinks.

---

[18] Ibid.

The dinner had proved a success and afterwards the group retired to the living room where coffee and brandy were served. On the horizon the Russian guns sounded a distant thunder.

Wallenberg was careful to face Eichmann and Krumey so that they were facing curtains that were covering an east-facing window. Eichmann sat in an overstuffed armchair, brandy snifter in hand. Then Wallenberg told Carlsson to open the curtains. Carlsson did so as Wallenberg turned the lights out. A fierce Soviet barrage lit the horizon to the east with explosives. Gote Carlsson, one of the guests at the dinner party was startled by the effect as the silhouettes in the room were lit up by the crackling gunfire.

"The effect was tremendous" Carlsson recalled. "The horizon was bright red from the fire of thousands of guns as the Russians closed in on Budapest."

Wallenberg stood at the window as Eichmann sat in his armchair, quaffing the brandy. He began to engage Eichmann in a conversation about National Socialism and the likely outcome of the war.

"It's not really a bona fide ideology," said Wallenberg. *"It's just the political incarnation of a single basic human emotion, hate.* How can it last?"

Eichmann tried to defend National Socialism spewing poisonous catchphrases about the Jewish-Bolshevik menace and world Jewish conspiracy.'

Fearlessly and brilliantly he (Wallenberg) picked Nazi doctrine apart, piece by piece, and foretold

73

the total defeat of its adherents. Wallenberg's intention was not so much to put his own views forward as to pass on a warning to Eichmann that he would do well to stop the deportation and extermination of Hungarian Jews.

Eichmann could scarcely conceal his amazement that anyone should dare to attack him and criticize the Fuhrer, but he soon seemed to realize that he was getting the worst of the argument. His propaganda phrases sounded hollow compared with Raoul's intelligent reasoning.

"Look how close the Bolsheviks are." Wallenberg told Eichmann. "Your war is almost over. Nazism is doomed, finished and so are those who cling to this hatred until the very last. It's the end of the Nazis and the end of Hitler."

"Finally, Eichmann said: 'I admit that you are right, Herr Wallenberg. I have never believed in Nazism, as such, but it has given me power and wealth. I know that this pleasant life of mine will soon be over. My planes will no longer bring me women and wine from Paris. My horses, my dogs, my luxurious quarters here in Budapest will soon be taken over by the Russians and I myself, as an SS officer, will be shot on the spot.

"For me there's no escape." added Eichmann. "There are, however, some consolations. If I continue to eliminate our enemies until the end, it may delay our defeat – even for just a few days. And then, when I finally do walk the gallows, at least I'll know I've completed my mission. (And) if I obey my orders from

Berlin and exercise my power harshly enough, I may prolong my respite for some time here in Budapest."

"Why don't you call off your people?' asked Wallenberg. "Why not leave now while you still can?"

Eichmann was beginning to lose his temper. "Budapest will be held as though it were Berlin." With that, Eichmann got up to leave. Then turned around to face his host.

"I want to thank you for an exceptionally charming and interesting evening." He said, shaking Wallenberg's hand.

"I warn you, therefore, Herr Legationssekretar, that I will do my best to stop you, and your Swedish diplomatic passport will not help you if I find it necessary to have you removed. Accidents do happen, even to a neutral diplomat."

With these menacing words, Eichmann stood up to leave, but not at all displaying any anger. With the imperturbable politeness of a well-educated German, he bade farewell to Raoul and thanked us for a particularly pleasant evening."[19]

---

[19] *Wallenberg* Danny Smith, 1986. Pp. 107 – 108. *The Envoy: The Epic Rescue of the Last Jews of Europe in the Desperate Closing Months of World War Two* Alex Kershaw, 2011, Pp. 118-119).

At the war's end, Wallenberg was captured and sent to Siberia where he disappeared behind the iron curtain in the Soviet gulags for the rest of his life. I have a hopeful picture in my mind that the memories of the tens of thousands of people he saved helped sustain him in the Siberian cold and isolation.

Joel Brand and Saly Mayer – "The Europa Plan."

"I am prepared to sell you one million Jews. Goods for blood – blood for goods. You can take them from any country you like, Hungary, Poland, the Ostmark, from Theresienstadt, from Auschwitz, wherever you like. I am willing to offer one hundred thousand Jews in advance, and a further ten percent on receipt of the first payment. 1,000 trucks in exchange for every 100,000 Jews. You are getting away cheap."[20]

Adolf Eichmann, negotiating with Joel Brand to 'sell' 1 million Jews on behalf of Himmler.

It is almost unimaginable to put a price tag on the value of human life. Yet Oscar Schindler, the famed industrialist, found a way to bribe a Nazi official to purchase the safety of his factory workers. This is also the strategy which saved thousands of Jews living in Slovakia and Hungary. It is a policy that might have saved millions more. As far-fetched as it sounds, the practice of ransoming Jews was a very real one among the Gestapo.

There are several examples of both successful negotiating for Jewish Lives and excruciatingly near-successes. Noting a German willingness to negotiate for Jewish lives in

---

[20] Donald Niewyk and Ian Kershaw, ed., *The Holocaust* (New York: Houghton Mifflin Co. 1997).

Slovakia in 1942 and Hungary in 1944, Joel Brand explored possibilities of ransoming Jews. He approached the Gestapo official in charge of exportation with a bribe of $50,000 to stop the deportation of 90,000 Jews. After sending the first half of the payment, the deportations stopped. But the international group of rabbis could not make the second deadline and four transports were sent to Poland. When the other $25,000 was raised the deportations were halted for another two years.[21]

Brand's efforts at first yielded results when Eichmann himself met with him and offered to ransom one million Jews for trucks, coffee and sugar supplies. In a terrible twist of fate, Brand was unable to convince nations, organizations or individuals of the legitimacy of the deal. He was detained and confronted with a bureaucracy and politicians whose priorities were elsewhere during the war and who placed little importance to the offer. This strikes me as criminally negligent indifference, to allow the imminent death of one million souls when a potential solution was at hand. After the invasion at Normandy, communication became difficult and the offer disappeared.

Another successful ransoming intervention example was the effort of Saly Mayer in Hungary.

> "Mayer, a Swiss citizen, was authorized to negotiate for the ransom of the Hungarian Jews in an attempt to gain time but not to offer to make any payments. He actually made a personal goodwill gesture of some Swiss tractors he bought to allow the talks to continue. In return, Himmler stopped the Budapest transports.

---

[21] Donald Niewyk and Ian Kershaw, ed., *The Holocaust* (New York: Houghton Mifflin Co. 1997), 270.

Through undaunted effort, Mayer tempted the Nazis to make some releases of Jews (1,200 from Thersienstadt) by showing he had access to $5 million in a Swiss bank account, controlled by the Americans."[22]

The two examples that follow are frightful. It is difficult to comprehend that a real possibility existed to stop the policy to exterminate the Jews during the height of the killing.

"A letter was sent through Wisliceny (Slovakian Gestapo) to Berlin on behalf of world Jewry the price Nazis had set for stopping all deportations throughout Europe. (Nov. 1942). The Nazis appeared to rise to the bait. After protracted negotiations, Wisleceny offered, in the name of his SS chiefs, to stop deportation from Western Europe and the Balkans for $2 million. Further negotiations on Poland and the actual Reich area might follow."[23]

The world Jewish Congress did not believe the deportations would stop and rejected the plan. They viewed the 'Europa Plan' as a blatant Nazi attempt to extort money. The fact remains that several deportations had been stopped through similar arrangements on the orders of a cash strapped Third Reich. While two million dollars may have aided the Nazi war machine, or more likely gone into the pockets of officials, it was insignificant compared to the lives it may have saved. It would have cost an unfathomable thirty to fifty cents per life saved, if this ransoming effort had been successful.

---

[22] Ibid., 271.
[23] Ibid., 273

Hungary adopted the same strategy to rescue its Jews, while escape routes to Slovakia and Romania were being forged. Toward the end of the war:

> "Eichmann himself ordered Brand to appear before him. He offered to release one million Jews (not only Jews of Hungary) in return for war material and other goods. In subsequent meetings the ransom became more specific: 10,000 trucks and quantities of coffee, tea, sugar and soap. The British, Americans and Russians refused him. It appears that the SS offer was serious. Because the Nazis believed the Jews controlled the West, they could be used as hostages. Their ransom might bring not only valuable war materials to a besieged Germany (this was the story Himmler 'sold' to Hitler) but might well move the Allies toward negotiating with the SS."[24]

The implications are staggering. Could these relatively innocuous deliveries have saved millions of lives? The fact that we can legitimately ask this question within the context of other successful efforts, highlights how many intervention opportunities exist, before and during genocide. These opportunities were present even in what has often been perceived as a monolithic, un-penetrable machine for extermination.

---

[24] Ibid., 274.

Bulgaria – Defying Hitler.

Bulgaria's leader King Boris, who was an ally of Hitler, is an example of how one individual's refusal could stop genocide in its inception and execution. Beyond this, it provides an insight of how a nation that has recently suffered acts of genocide itself (Bulgaria at the hands of Turkey) can have a pronounced and widespread sympathy for others being persecuted and massacred.

Bulgaria government gave some concessions to the Third Reich on Jewish policies, but categorically refused to turn over their Jewish population for deportation. "The plan to persecute the Jews was met with widespread opposition from every corner of the nation. It was strange to point out the dangers of a small number of Jews (50,000) when there were 650,000 Turks (in Bulgaria)."[25]

Bulgaria's refusal to deport their Jews was largely because anti-Semitism was practically non-existent there. Another factor may be that Bulgaria had suffered ethnic massacres at the hands of the Turks in recent years. Is it possible that their more humane policy toward the Jews could be the result of their suffering under similar circumstances? The memory of innocent unarmed Bulgarian villagers being cut down was still fresh in their national psyche. To appease the Reich they passed a few restrictive laws, for example: no Jews could have gentile servants, there were limits on the number of Jews in certain professions, Jews could not send money out of the country, there was a 20% Jewish tax, they were not allowed

[25] Marshall Lee Miller, *Bulgaria During the Second World War*. (San Francisco: Stanford University Press, 1975), 96.

to own or possess radios, and Jews were required to wear the Star of David (which few did)."[26] The Minister of the Interior went to the Jews when they protested his decision. He asked them to be patient and explained that the worst was over. Adolph Eichmann, the Nazi officer in charge of the 'final solution' was frustrated by the Bulgarian intransigence He began chipping away by having them allow Bulgarian Jews living abroad or in newly acquired territory to be deported to the camps. Then his representative finally threatened Bulgarian King Boris and he relented and signed the document to allow the Nazis to relocate the entire Bulgarian Jews to the East. Days later, with the pressure off, the King rescinded his decision and the Bulgarian Jews were to be safe until the end of the war.[27]

The newly acquired land of Macedon and Thrace, however, were deemed to be technically out of the national boundaries of the State of Bulgaria, even though they were under Bulgarian administration. Over 11,000 of these Jews were deported directly by the SS and killed. Late in the war, German operatives rounded up the Sophia Jews and sent them to the countryside to await deportation. But through the stalling of the Bulgarian government, this (the deportation) never occurred.[28]

King Boris attempted to get permission to send his Jews to British Palestine. The expense would have been great, due to the German fees to allow this to occur. Ultimately, British

---

[26] Ibid., 96.
[27] Mark Mazower, *Inside Hitler's Greece* (New haven, Yale University Press, 1993) 241.
[28] Ibid., 242.

Foreign Minister Aden blocked the effort.[29] King Boris would oppose Hitler one more time, in a contentious meeting in August of 1943 where Hitler pressured him for troops to oppose the Soviets and to change his Jewish deportation policy. King Boris refused. Two weeks later he was dead shortly after a dinner at the Italian Embassy where, many believed, he was poisoned at the behest of Hitler for opposing his Jewish policy and refusing him troops.

Denmark – Widespread Rescue of Jews.

The Danes had two factors to aid in a credible campaign to oppose to the Third Reich policy of extermination of Jews: strong leadership and favorable geography. In Denmark, King Christian X led the effort to smuggle the Danish Jews to safety and was an important factor in motivating his people. The fall of Denmark to German forces on April 9th, 1940, in six hours, remains one of the quickest military defeats in history. In part, because of this swift and relatively painless fall of Denmark to Germany, the government of Denmark was left largely intact.[30] This was an essential factor of the ability of the society to mobilize the effort to help the Jewish population escape unharmed to Sweden.

The Danish policy on deportation was that the government simply refused to give up their Jewish citizens.

---

[29] *A History of Israel from the Rise of Zionism to Our Time.* Howard M. Sachar, Knopf, New York, 2007

[30] Michael Marrus and Robert O. Paxton, "Western Europeans and the Jews," in *The Holocaust* (New York: Houghton Mifflin Co., 1997), 100.

Denmark was not treated as oppressively and with as much manpower as other Nazi-conquered nations, in part because Danish loyalty to the Third Reich was assumed by the Nazis due to their Germanic/Nordic heritage. This less strict oversight may partially explain the success of their effort to rescue Jews to neutral Sweden. Then during the summer of 1943, in the middle of a turbulent year, the Nazis attempted to forcibly take the Jews for deportation. In a mix of defiance to the Reich authority and humanitarian concern, Danish individuals, the government and neutral third-party agencies such as the Red Cross, all helped to transfer most of the Jewish community to neutral Sweden and safety. It was largely successful, though the Nazis were able to intercept 475 of the 8,000 fleeing Jews.[31] This is one of the most outstanding examples of how unified resistance through strong national and individual leadership can save lives in the most daunting of circumstances. A nation that was conquered in six hours was morally strong enough to save over 94% of their Jews.

The Wannsee Conference.

On January 20th, 1942, fifteen men convened a meeting in a beautiful countryside mansion. The delicious foods and wine were in sharp contrast to the deprivations of the war raging around them. They gathered to enact the 'final solution' of all Jews of Europe and the U.S.S.R. No longer would the Jews emigrate, stay in camped ghettos or be massacred in relatively small numbers by gun or in 'gas vans' that roamed the countryside killing standing Jewish passengers with exhaust

---

[31] Ibid., 104.

fumes. Thirteen of the fifteen present immediately embraced the plan outlined by Reinhart Heydrich and his number two, Adolf Eichmann. All Jews were to be deported to Auschwitz where an industrial production-line of death was being built. There they would go into showers which were actually gas chambers, to be poisoned to death by zyklon B and their bodies burned in industrial crematoriums leaving practically no trace of the person, and the race, that existed before.

Before the end of the meeting, all fifteen agreed on the solution. One transcript of the meeting survived and outlines the gruesome efficiency of these monsters of humanity. Their plan was put into effect almost immediately and the killing machine peaked from 1943-45 decimating more than five million Jews and millions more Slavs, Gypsies, Communists, political prisoners, homosexuals, clergy, captured soldiers and other innocents. The industrial death camp of Auschwitz could murder 2500 per hour, 60,000 per day. Barely an objection arose around the table, with the exception of some political infighting. Alternatives to mass slaughter were briefly discussed including sterilization but none seriously. Dr Wilhelm Stuckart argued against the dismantling of the Nuremburg race Laws that he co-authored but relented. Of the 15 men who attended the Wannsee 'final solution' conference, five survived the war.

Of these five men who survived the war, only Adolf Eichmann was executed for his crimes. The rest lived long, relatively normal lives, some were successful in business and life, and were never punished for the millions of lives they were responsible for murdering. They lived without the stigma or punishment of being the brain trust of one of the worst genocides the world had ever known.

The Cold War Genocides 1965 – 1979.
Indonesia, China, Ibo, Bangladesh and Cambodia.

Indonesia 1965.

> "The fact that a man is a man is more important
> than the fact that he believes what he believes."
> John Hersey.[32]

The vast majority of people killed for ideological reasons in the past one hundred years, perished under communist or fascist regimes. Indonesia, however, offers a good counterexample of a country in which communist party members (P.K.I.) and their families were specifically targeted and massacred.

The Indonesian massacres of communists in 1965-66 killed between 300,000 to 500,000 people according to conservative estimates. These massacres were largely carried out by army units and vigilante militia groups with strong political affiliations. A communist coup attempt in 1965 set off the explosive situation. The reaction to the near coup was a massacre of communist party members and their families ordered by the general who has survived the coup attempt.[33] The reaction of the world was almost non-existent. As word of

---

[32] Irving Louis Horowitz, *Taking Lives: Genocide and State Power*. (New Brunswick: Transaction Publishers, 1997), 69.

[33] Robert Cribb, "The Indonesian Massacres," in *Century of Genocide* (New York: Garland Publishing, 1997), 237.

the ideological genocides of the U.S.S.R had been suppressed, so too had word of the Indonesian massacres disappeared. Few of us in the West have ever heard of the Indonesian or Bangladeshi genocides. This arises from: the inaccessibility of the area, an ideologically charged climate and an emerging dictator who was willing to perpetrate genocide for political advantage, while his allies looked the other way.

China 1966 – 1976.

After a disastrous agrarian reform policy which cost over twenty million lives, China's communist dictator Mao's leadership position was in jeopardy. In the early 1960s he rocketed back to popularity due to his book, 'Mao's Red Book of Quotations.' The zeal with which the youth embraced his concept of perpetual revolution, led the youth to target many of Mao's political enemies and stabilize his place firmly at the head of Chinese leadership again. During this time, millions of Chinese were beaten, tortured, re-socialized, trained to purge themselves of capitalistic thought. Hundreds of thousands died as a result, and palpable fear ran through China during this period of purges. While the Chinese purges were not as brutal or as all-consuming as Stalin's Soviet purges of the 1930s, it devastated millions of lives and families and sapped an ancient civilization of its potential as other world players advanced on the world stage. The 'counter revolutionary' purges ended with Mao's death in 1976 and the eventual rise of Deng, a comparative reformer, in 1978.

The Ibo of Nigeria (Biafra) 1967 - 1970.

In 1967, the Ibo of Nigeria exercised their right to self-determination and declared their independence. The new nation was called Biafra from an ancient name for the area. It separated itself from a Nigeria that was fraught with military dictatorships, political assassinations, and coups. Nigeria has over 350 languages and dialects, three major ethnicities and dozens of minor ethnicities, and two major religions. The war for independence began to go badly for the Ibo when the Nigerian government chose to attack the Ibo food supply and starve the fledgling nation into submission rather than to defeat them militarily. This strategy has been used with the Native American Sioux (1876-7), Ukraine (1932-3), the Nuba of Sudan (2002, 2011), Zimbabwe (2002) and North Korea (2002).

Bangladesh 1971.

One of the least discussed full-scale genocides is the wanton slaughter of Bangladeshis in 1971 by the Pakistani army. It is believed that a staggering 3 million Bangladeshis perished, 10 million were displaced to India, 30 million were internally displaced and 250,000 women were raped in a nine month period of time.[34] The cause of the massacres lay in the Pakistani government's attempt to keep Bangladesh as a part of

---

[34] Rounaq Jahan, "Genocide in Bangladesh," in *Century of Genocide* (New York: Garland Publishing, 1997), 291.

Pakistan. When India gained its independence and broke up, the Muslim Bangladeshis willingly joined in a union with the Pakistanis. It soon became apparent that the union was not to their benefit. Politically and economically the Pakistanis dominated the union without regard for the Bengalis. When the Bengalis began to move for independence in 1971, the Pakistani Yahya regime sent in the army. 'Operation Searchlight' headed by General Khan of Pakistan was responsible for the massive killing and rape that followed, which appalled the international community and galvanized the Bangladeshi Muslims. It took many months before smuggled videos were able to make it to Western media to be broadcast, the first revealing the massacres at Dhaka University. The backdrop to this genocide was, once again, the Cold War. Pakistan was aligned with the U.S while India, and eventually Bangladesh, were Soviet aligned. Did this Cold War alliance play a role in the under reporting of this genocide in the West?

Ultimately the intervention of the Indian army, at the behest of its President Indira Gandhi, combined with Bangladeshi forces defeated the Pakistani forces, stopped the genocide and Bangladesh gained its independence.

Cambodia 1975 - 1979.

> "Saloth Sar would not have killed a chicken."
>
> A neighbor who knew
> (Pol Pot) as a youth.[35]

After the failure of Mao's Great Leap Forward (1958 – 1961), which cost approximately twenty million lives when people starved due to the collectivization of China's farms, Pol Pot's Khmer Rouge believed that Mao's failure was because he had not gone far enough with his reforms. They believed that the Khmer State (call Kampuchea at the time) should first tear everything down and start at the beginning, at 'year zero.' Toward that end, the Khmer Rouge emptied the cities of people and forced almost the entire Cambodian population into the countryside. The Khmer Rouge taught their captive nation that family ties were counter revolutionary, as was an education and books and they proceeded to kill one out of every three Cambodians in five years. That was 2,400,000 of 7,100,000 people, in an attempt to teach their vision.[36] What was their vision? The creation of a peasant-based agrarian society, one which was anti-intellectual, anti-family and anti-urban. This was a revolution where you could be killed because you wore glasses because it was a sign you were an intellectual.

During the revolution, children who turned on their parents and family were particularly prized and often were elevated in rank at teen and pre-teen years.

---

[35] Ben Kiernan, "The Cambodian Genocide," in *Century of Genocide* (New York: Garland Publishing, 1997), 335.
[36] *Statistics of Democide: Ch 4: Statistics of Cambodian Genocide* Charlottesville, 1997. RJ Rummel.

"In the first few weeks after Cambodia fell to the Khmer Rouge in April 1975, the nation's cities were evacuated, hospitals emptied, schools closed, factories deserted, money and wages abolished...Freedom of press, movement, worship, organization and discussion completely disappeared for nearly four years. So did everyday family life. A whole nation was kidnapped, and then besieged from within. Meals had to be eaten in collective mess halls...it was a prison camp state, and (of the 8 million prisoners)... 1.5 million were worked, starved and beaten to death."[37]

The absolute power with which Pol Pot and his Khmer Rouge ruled Cambodia left the nation utterly silent. No word seeped out of the country. Buddhist monasteries were targeted for annihilation. Two hundred thousand Vietnamese who lived in Cambodia ceased to exist by 1979. Approximately half had fled the country and the rest, almost down to the individual, were murdered. Half the Chinese population (425,000) were annihilated, as well as almost forty percent of the Muslim Cham communities.[38] By targeting specific ethnic groups for extermination the Khmer Rouge fulfilled the technical requirements for the UN Genocide Convention definition of genocide, but ideological or political genocide was their

---

[37] Ibid., 334.
[38] Ibid., 340-341.

clearest intention. The ultimate irony is that it was the Communist government of Vietnam, which was itself guilty of internal purges, and egregious human rights abuse, that finally ended the Cambodian genocide.

The damage of this genocide to Cambodian society is still felt and seen to this day. With the inexplicable death of such a large amount of its population at the hands of some that are still living among them, Cambodia has chosen to try to ignore this horrible chapter in its history, and to bury it, rather than to confront it and heal it. Part of the reason for this was the continued existence of the Khmer Rouge as a military force until recently.

Sierra Leone 1991 – 2002. A Generation Without Limbs.

"The soldiers would come up to you with machetes in their hands and ask you: "Long sleeve, or short sleeve?" If you said short sleeve they would push you down, hold you to a table or tree stump and chop off your arm near the elbow. If you said long sleeve, they would shop your hand off at the wrist."

> Eddie Turay, former Presidential candidate in Sierra Leone discussing RUF mutilations.

The Eddie Turay Story – Long Sleeve, Short Sleeve?

When I was attempting to found the Center for the Prevention of Genocide, I had assembled the prospective Board of Directors and invited two speakers who had suffered genocide personally to come speak. Eddie Turay was the second of them.

He lumbered into the board room. He was a large, broad shouldered African man from Sierra Leone who approached the lectern. Eddie Turay had been a presidential candidate for the All African People's Congress Party in Sierra Leone before the war broke out. When the war overran his hometown, he was

93

captured. He told about seeing the hated rebels, the RUF, tossing babies up in the air and catching them with their blades. He told of a popular game that the RUF rebels would play. They would pull a pregnant woman roughly out of line and bet on her.

"25 Leones, it's a boy."

"No man, 50, it's a girl."

"Okay 50."

They would then cut her open and the baby would spill out and one would win the bet and the mother and baby died on the spot. True horror.

Eddie told about how he escaped death through a bizarre mistake of identity. He was rounded up and sent to prison. After a few days they called out the names of approximately fifty known political leaders. These leaders were to step from their cells and marched to the center of the courtyard. Eddie stayed in his cell. He hoped against common sense that they wouldn't notice that he wasn't there. For some inexplicable reason they didn't. Maybe the person who took his place thought that the political leaders were being released so he took Eddie's place. Whatever the reason, the RUF prison guards counted them. The correct number of prisoners was outside. They shot them on the spot. None survived.

He told stories about the procedures the RUF employed to intimidate and take revenge. They were punishing everyone for voting in the recent election which they had boycotted. If you go today to Sierra Leone, you will find tens of thousands of people who are missing hands and arms.

"The soldiers would come up to you with machetes in their hands and ask you. Long sleeve, or short sleeve? An innocent enough sounding question. If you said short sleeve they would push you down, hold you to a table or tree stump and chop off your arm near the elbow. Sometimes they would take both arms. If you said long sleeve, they would shop your hand off at the wrist."

Edward eventually secured his release from prison and made a risky attempt to escape the country. At the border a few days later, a husky, quite manly looking, six foot one, woman, wearing a dress that barely fit her, crossed the border. It was Eddie Turay's first leg of his journey to safety.

The most enduring impression of the war in Sierra Leone is the sight of men, women and children, from the east and west, lining up and to have their limbs cut off. This was as a Revolutionary United Front (RUF) punishment for areas that voted when rebel leader Foday Sankoh had warned the country to boycott the election. This gruesomeness applied to little children as well. There were massacres and other unspeakable acts of barbarity, but the primary characteristic was the disfigurement of a generation.

The highlight of this conflict was the struggle over the lucrative diamond mines in the North. Liberia's President Charles Taylor supported the vicious RUF and benefitted from their control of the mines. Child warriors were used on the RUF side and eventually the government side as well. The British took an interest as the former colony but was confronted with the grim reality that victory involved killing a number of these children warriors in order to disarm the RUF. In this dilemma, the British came up with a unique solution. They hired 'Executive Outcomes' to dislodge the rebel control of the diamond area. While not conclusive, the use of mercenaries did prove effective in this particular conflict. The loss of a large part of their income left the RUF in a more vulnerable position and the British and government forces eventually defeated them. Charles Taylor of Liberia was tried and convicted for war crimes by the I.C.C and RUF leader Foday Sankoh was indicted prior to his death.

There are several salient lessons to be taken away from Sierra Leone's civil war. The first is that there is no end to human depravity. This conflict has child soldiers on both sides, permanent bodily mutilation as a standard form of abuse of bystanders, massacres, and greed. Second, mercenary forces, which are known professional entities beholden to the Geneva and other applicable International Conventions, *may* be a viable option for some of the more complex human rights abuse scenarios which require military intervention. Lastly, in my view, the healing that took place in Sierra Leone and the role of women in that process after the horror was over, was key as well. In Ishmael Beah's book *A Long Way Gone* and in the many interviews subsequent to its release, he credits his recovery from the post-traumatic stress of being a child soldier on his adoptive parents:

> "To get over it, it took the action of selfless people, adults, who were willing to see us as kids and treat us as kids and love us with a depth of compassion that it allowed us to move past what we had seen and done."[39]

---

[39] Ishmael Beah. *A Long Way Gone.*

We know that mankind is talented at destroying, waging war and committing atrocities. We also know that mankind is learning how to creatively solve those issues and put the pieces together of the lives it effected.

Rwanda 1994.

> "People became fools. I don't know why. I kept telling them, 'I don't agree with what you're doing,' just as openly as I'm telling you now. I'm a man who's used to saying no when I have to. That's all I did - what I felt like doing. Because I never agree with killers. I didn't agree with them. I refused, and I told them so."

> Paul Rusesabagina

My interest in nationalism and genocide came from my Armenian heritage. I always wondered how the Armenian genocide could have occurred in full view of the world community without being stopped. Although almost a century ago, it was a defining moment in my family's history. An explanation for this worldwide phenomenon of indifference to genocide occurred to me after the Rwandan genocide took place. In 1994, when the Rwandan genocide occurred, I read U.S newspaper coverage of it hidden beneath the O.J Simpson's trial and thought 'what a shame' and turned to the rest of the newspaper. I had no connection with Rwanda. I wasn't Tutsi, my identities were American, Irish, Italian and Armenian. None of those were being massacred so the impetus for action did not exist in me. It was three years later when I began to research genocide at Georgetown that the subtle danger of nationalism began to occur to me. Because of my lack of connection to those victims of genocide in Rwanda, their humanity was unconsciously and automatically assigned a lesser amount of value to me. Was this not the same phenomenon that occurred to my ancestors as the world failed to respond to their massacre? This is a common and dangerous tendency that still exists today. There are several answers for how to solve this, but it requires action from people like you and me, who are not, and will never be, in jeopardy, to help bring about the solution.

At the end of the Nineteenth Century and the beginning of the Twentieth Century, Armenians were being massacred and the world watched in horror but could do nothing. At the end of the Twentieth Century the world watched Rwanda with disinterest as Tutsis were massacred and chose to do nothing to stop it. Between these two genocides there had been dozens of full-scale, military-sponsored and man-made famine-based genocides. The world was no longer surprised. But the Rwandan genocide is perhaps the most devastating and frustrating because it was so detectable and preventable. Rwanda clearly showed that the world was no closer to preventing genocide than it was one hundred years earlier.

Unsurprisingly, news and other items of interest in the world newspapers eclipsed the genocide in the little known land of Rwanda. In Africa, the headlines focused on the democratization of South Africa and difficulties in Somalia. In Europe, the Bosnian War was raging and the First Chechen War had begun. In the United States, the O.J. Simpson trial reigned supreme and relegated the important issue of the Tutsi genocide to the back pages of most newspapers. Many who were familiar with the situation in Rwanda assumed the disturbance, after the assassination of President Habyarimana, was part of the confusing instability of the region. Few outside Rwanda realized, at the outset, that what was happening was a carefully planned genocide.[40] Few outsiders anticipated that one million people would lose their lives within the next one hundred days. But the few who did know were in strong positions to prevent or mitigate the genocide.

The history of Hutu and Tutsi massacres dates back to colonial times. In the year 1972 alone, over 100,000 Hutus living in Burundi were massacred, in response to a Hutu attempt to seize control of the Burundi government. The Hutu were, indiscriminately, slaughtered regardless of age and sex. In 1988, between 5,000-20,000 Hutus were massacred by the Tutsi-dominated Burundi army. The initial Hutu attempted coup in 1972 had targeted innocent Tutsi men, women and children and the Tutsi response was similarly ugly and wildly disproportionate. These actions were certainly precursors to the full-scale Rwandan genocide of the Tutsis in 1994 at the hands of the Hutus. In fact, some of the perpetrators of the 1994 genocide were survivors of the 1988 massacres.

The Rwandan genocide is distinct from other genocides in that, though initiated by an ethnic political clique trying to remain in power, Rwanda's genocide had the ground swell of popular support from non-targeted citizens. While this was clearly planned from the top, it was carefully orchestrated to encourage average Hutus to help the militia kill the Tutsi. The planners attempted to legitimize the behavior through the idea that "If everybody is implicated, then implication becomes meaningless."[8] After a successful radio campaign vilifying the Tutsi, many average Hutus were swept into the killing frenzy.

---

[40] Fergal Keane, *A Season of Blood: A Rwandan Journey*. (New York: Viking Press, 1995), 7.

After the assassination of President Habyarimana, the sizable Presidential guard and massive Hutu militias, aided by the government executed a long-planned campaign of extermination against the Tutsi minority in Rwanda.

> "Following the militias' example, Hutus' young and old rose to the task. Neighbors hacked neighbors to death in their homes, and colleagues hacked colleagues to death in their workplace. Doctors killed their patients, and schoolteachers killed their pupils."[41]

If a massive number of Hutu were guilty of crimes of genocide, we, the world community, were the neutral third parties who were guilty of passive complicity. A picture comes to mind of German citizens being to look at the concentration camps to force the realization of their passive complicity in the Holocaust. The Rwandan genocide had been predicted and could have been prevented. Just prior to the beginning of the massacres in January, Canadian Brigadier General Dallaire sent a fax to the UN Peacekeeping Headquarters with a very specific warning of the impending genocide. An informant had given Dallaire information about the intentions of the Hutu elite. These intentions included the provocation and massacre of the Belgian UN troops and the registration of all Tutsi for their extermination. The informant noted that the Hutu militia were

---

[41] [8]Philip Gourevitch, *We Wish to Inform You That Tomorrow We Will Be Killed With Our Families*. (New York: Farrar Straus and Giroux, 1998), 115.

trained and capable of killing up to 1,000 Tutsi within twenty minutes. The fax was ignored and General Dallaire was told to hand over his informer to the proper authorities. Everything predicted in that fax transpired exactly as the informer had foretold. The chief of peacekeeping operations was none other than Kofi Annan the future Secretary General of the UN.[42] On April 7th, the day after President Habyarimana's assassination, Belgian UN peacekeepers arrived at the residence of the Rwandan Prime Minister.

> "The Prime Minister fled over her garden wall
> and was killed nearby. Before the Belgians
> could leave, a Rwandan officer drove up and
> ordered them to surrender their arms and come
> with him. The Belgians, outnumbered, were
> taken to Camp Kigali where they were held for
> several hours, then tortured, murdered, and
> mutilated."[12]

The killing of the Belgian peacekeepers precipitated a large UN withdrawal. But during the first weeks of violence, the UN peacekeeping force of 2,000 soldiers was present in Rwanda. It was soon reduced to less than 200, contrary to General Dallaire's recommendation. This was due to the political concern of those nations who had peacekeepers stationed there. General Dallaire strenuously objected to the withdrawal of troops and petitioned for an increased presence in Rwanda as the killing began to unfold. The General promised that with five thousand UN soldiers he could immediately halt

---

[42] Ibid., 105.

the genocide. The world sat and waited while the UN Security Council debated what to do. What followed was then, and remains now, a dark stain on the reputation of the UN. The UN voted to reduce its forces in Rwanda by 90%. Embassies closed and foreigners were quickly evacuated from the country, leaving the Tutsi remained to face massacre. In the Security Council, the United States had insisted that the events in Rwanda should not be considered a genocide. Politically, there were several missions underway including the costly Bosnian mission and the unpopular Somalian mission. Ultimately, influenced by the US, the Security Council failed to consider Rwanda a genocide and thus UN members were not compelled to act under law. Had they deemed the Rwandan genocide to be what it was, in fact, the Security Council would have been required under international law to respond.

In few instances the killing was temporarily stemmed. In one case the *prefect* was a Tutsi who refused to allow the massacre of his countrymen. He was soon replaced by a Hutu extremist who pursued the task of genocide with vengeful efficiency. The entire structure of Rwandan government, from the national to the local, played active roles in the genocide, with almost no exception. The efficiency of the massacres is a testimony to this horrible fact. When the Tutsis tried to flee, they were immediately executed as they reached the borders. Many local populations, poisoned by the radio broadcasts and fueled by hate and greed, turned on the native Tutsi population with a viciousness which has few parallels in modern history. The number of bodies was so great that garbage trucks were used to clear the towns of bodies.

The international community had not learned from the past, but by knowing the UN did not have the stomach to intervene, the perpetrators showed that they had learned from the history of genocide. In actuality, some of the international community did clamor for an immediate intervention. Czechoslovakia, New Zealand, Spain and several African nations spearheaded a movement to force a humanitarian intervention almost immediately following the UN withdrawal. The eight-member African group which wanted to intervene requested fifty armored personnel carriers to help prevent casualties. The US delayed on this issue, finally agreeing to lend the carriers for a price of 15 million dollars. "Meanwhile the armored personnel carriers sat on a runway in Germany while the UN pleaded for a five million dollar reduction of the rental charge"[43] They remained there until after the killing was over. Ultimately the Rwandan Patriotic Front, a highly disciplined multi-ethnic force, reclaimed most of Rwanda. When the UN finally sanctioned the French-led 'Operation Turquoise,' the killing of the Tutsis continued in those areas that the French had secured! R.P.F advance finally ended the genocide.

There were individuals who simply stood up during the genocide and saved lives without compromising. Paul Rusesebegina, of 'Hotel Rwanda' fame used the valuable commodity of beer to forestall the persecution of his refugee guests. When the situation became grave, he used every political contact, alcohol and money to save the refugees from being evicted from his hotel to their certain death.

It is ironic that the West, which traditionally places a high regard on the sanctity of individual rights, while hundreds of thousands of those individuals were massacred, gave more

---

[43] Ibid.,

media attention to the trial of former U.S. football player O.J Simpson. One American celebrity's trial eclipsed the life and death struggle of almost one million, non-American men, women and children. Are the Tutsi mothers, fathers, sons and daughters less beautiful, less pertinent, less valuable by virtue of their foreign-ness? Was it their foreign-ness that allowed their massacre to become just a footnote in our American daily lives? Our lack of connection to them made us regard them in less than human terms.

We are inoculated to the horrors of genocide, numbed to them because they have become commonplace. Reading accounts such as the following, it is a wonder how we can turn a deaf ear to this horror simply because we have heard it before.

> "As I walk towards the gate, I must make a detour to avoid the bodies of several people. There is a child who has been decapitated and there are three other corpses splayed on the ground. A woman on her side, an expression of surprise on her face, her mouth open and a deep gash in her head. She is wearing a red cardigan and a blue dress."[44]

The Red Cross officially put the death toll in Rwanda at over one million. The UN withdrew its peacekeeping force following the death of ten Belgian peacekeepers.

After the reality of the genocide was revealed, the world reaction, was impressive. The world community

---

[44] [21]Keane Fergal, *A Season of Blood: A Rwandan Journey.* (New York: Viking Press, 1995), 78

launched the largest relief effort by the international humanitarian aid industry of the Twentieth Century, an effort which would have been entirely unnecessary had early warning been heeded with the rapid response to intervene. We are remarkable at sending many firefighters after the house has burned to the ground.

In the immediate aftermath of the Rwandan genocide, Hutu perpetrators fled with the millions of refugees to D R Congo. There they massacred 39,000 Congolese Tutsis called Banyamulenge. Killings occurred in the refugee camps as well.

The very thin silver lining for Rwanda was the 'Gacaca' traveling court that went throughout Rwanda seeking perpetrators to come out publicly and confess and ask for forgiveness of the victims in the community. This courts functioned similar to the 'truth and reconciliation' efforts of South Africa which was occurring around the same time. It promoted healing, and conflict prevention to diffuse the cycle of vengeance likely to occur after trauma where neighbors killed neighbors. While divisions still are present in Rwanda today, the role the 'Gacaca' courts played in helping Rwanda move past the genocide is indisputable.

Bosnia and Kosovo 1994 and 1999.
Ajsha's Story

Her sister said: "Sister, let's pray sister." 'So we prayed for a miracle.'

Ajsha Pllana as machine guns were pointed at them as they knelt.

Ajsha's Story.

During one of my last human rights classes at University of South Florida, I was not sure that she would arrive. Fifteen minutes after the beginning of class Ajsha entered quietly, gracefully, sporting a bright bubblegum pink spring dress that was at odds with the discussion about to take place. She turned a little red as she slowly began her story.   Her   father   had been a Professor at the University for many years and had taught many students, sometimes taking them home to tutor them, free of charge, at his kitchen table, as his wife cooked dinner. It was after the Bosnian War that Yugoslav President Milosevic started a campaign to replace ethnically Albanian teachers and civil servants with Serbs. Her father lost his job at the University.

Ajsha woke up in the middle of the night to screams. Her town was located on a lake surrounded by mountains and sound could echo throughout the lake. She ran to her parents' room and told her mother she heard screams. Her mother assured her it was just some Serbian soldiers who were drinking and their voices had carried.

The next morning the town was evacuated. Serbian

107

forces watched by NATO observers were ethnically cleansing the village. Ajsha and her family carefully stepped around the bodies of the villagers who were massacred and laid in the streets. Most Kosovars were numb to this scene, but Ajsha remembered how a NATO soldier cried at the sight of the bodies of the late night massacre.

The Pllana family went into hiding with friends at a nearby village. For several months they stayed in a basement, mostly reading, sometimes learning or playing games, rarely ever coming out and then only at night to stretch their legs and breathe in some fresh air. Several months later their friend rushed into the basement and told them 'You have to go, now. They're checking attics and basements and finding people!'

The Professor and Mrs. Pllana had discussed their strategy several times and concluded that trying to leave the country across to Macedonia was too risky. Three young girls and a young attractive mother would be an easy target for the Serbian militias known for rape and they controlled access to the Macedonian border. So they came up with an improbable but potentially good plan. They would go home. They would return to their home in their village which was now abandoned. They had canned food stored and they could stay hidden at home indefinitely until the trouble was over. No one would ever think to look for them in the evacuated town.

They went unseen for the whole trip back and were in their final approach, the last three blocks to their home, hurrying through an open park area, when they saw the car. It was a Yugo. It skittered by them on the nearest street, with its engine making a tinny whirring sound, one block away from the park. It was parallel to them, then past them. Maybe they didn't see them. Then the Yugo slammed on its brakes and backed up.

The Pllanas froze in their tracks in the middle of the green grass. Four men lumbered out of the Yugo carrying machine guns and yelling at them to halt.

The irregular militia men barked an order for papers. They didn't dare show them the real ones or they would be shot on the spot so Professor Pllana started making elaborate searching gestures through his pockets and Mrs. Pllana started to berate him for always forgetting his papers, hoping that the theater they were performing was convincing. Then Ajsha panicked. She knew they were dead. The nine year old blanched and ran blindly. The alarmed men threatened to shoot her if her sister didn't catch her. Her sister ran to her, caught her by the arm and said: 'Sister, let's pray.'

They kneeled and prayed to be delivered from death when the militiaman standing behind the others stepped out and asked: 'Professor Pllana?' They recognized the young man immediately. Professor Pllana had failed him as a student several years before. But then, as was his habit, Professor Pllana took him to his home and tutored him at the kitchen table and he ate dinner with the family, many times, until he passed Professor Pllana's class.

"It's okay, their okay. I'll take care of this." His student said to his unit. Then he took Professor Pllana by the arm and motioned for the rest of the family to follow. 'Where are you going? Do you live close? Show me the house and I'll make sure no one troubles you. But you must never come out."

And so the Pllana family survived. Eventually they were to cross the Macedon border successfully. They stayed in a refugee camp and then immigrated to the United States. Professor Pllana died some years ago. The sisters and mother have gone on to a happy, successful life in the United States.

To me, the author, Ajsha Pllana is the unlikely face of genocide. Young, vibrant and deserving of protection.

The first move toward the disintegration of Yugoslavia during the end of the Cold War, came from Slovenia. With a 97% ethnically Slovene population, the separation from Yugoslavia was relatively quick and painless. When Croatia followed in 1991, the time for peaceful separation was over. Deep scars from the Second World War resurfaced with memories of how the Serb population, previously trapped under fascist Croatian rule in the Krajina, had been persecuted and sent to concentration camps. There were Serbian minorities spread throughout the other Yugoslav Republics and Serbs sought to protect them from the persecution they suffered under Croatian hands during World War Two, and even Muslim hands before then. The Serbians quickly used the Yugoslavian military might to attempt to keep Bosnia and Croatia in the union and protect Serbians in the disputed territories. After arming and securing the Serbian-dominated territory of the Krajina in Croatia, and large portions of Serbian-controlled Bosnian territory, their protective military campaign soon turned into something much worse.

Attempted Interventions and other Possibilities. Allied attempts to mediate and redraw the borders to curtail the ongoing conflict were well-intentioned but fatally half-hearted. Former NATO commander Colin Powell explained logically that no forces should be committed unless victory was possible, sending the unmistakable signal that America's heart was not in the Balkan struggle. Without being able to rely on the force of NATO's major sponsoring member, potential aggressors on all sides of the conflict saw no reason to take the inflexible negotiation terms seriously. "We don't have a dog in that fight," was the way US Secretary of State James A. Baker described American interest in the area. The message was clear. The terms of any agreement would not be backed up by an enforcing power. This fuzzy-minded, vague inaction constitutes fatal and inexcusable indifference. The lessons of disengagement and appeasement prior to World War Two had been long forgotten.

One look at the ethnic map of Yugoslavia puts into perspective the reason why Slovenia would leave peacefully, but Bosnia and Croatia, without negotiations and reformed borders, would leave only through conflict. Bosnia is the very picture of a mixed ethnicity federal nation. Which works well until forces are present which demand its breakup. But if you try to break Bosnia apart, the opposite of indifference needs to occur, great care needs to be applied. One can see form the map the reason Bosnia was the site of most of the Bosnian War.

45

---

45 CIA World Factbook 1998, Appendices.

Once the mass atrocities of the Yugoslavian soldiers had come to light, including the massacre of over 9,000 Muslim men and boys at Srebrenica, NATO finally woke from its torpor and intervened. A massive bombing campaign ensued which paralyzed practically all Serbian military movement. President Clinton assigned Assistant Secretary of State Richard Holbrooke to lead negotiations in a hard hitting, tough session between Slobodon Milosevic, Franjo Tudman and Alija Izetbegovic on a US military base in Dayton, Ohio. One participant later said they felt like the US would not let them go home unless they came to an agreement to end the war. Agree they did. And the Bosnian War ended with the signing of the Dayton Agreement in December 1995.

In 1999, Ajsha Pllana's family and thousands like them began to flee from the first massacres and Serbian ethnic cleansing of Kosovo. Milosevic had long made the dubious claim that the Serbian minority in Kosovo had been abused by the Muslim, ethnically Albanian, Kosovars. For years Milosevic had forced laws on the small enclave that elevated Serbians and removed Albanians from key positions throughout Kosovo. In several instances, Kosovo Serbians loyal to Milosevic would serve as his proxy throughout what was left of Yugoslavia, storming to any city that Milosevic needed a spontaneous show of strength or support. Under the same pretext of abuse of the Serbian minority, Milosevic invaded Kosovo with regular army and militia to ethnically cleanse the province of Muslims/Albanians. The massacres began almost immediately.

It did not take long this time for the vigilant US Secretary of State Madeleine Albright to utilize satellite imagery of the area to pinpoint mass grave sites. In March 1999,

Finnish forensics specialists confirmed the discovery of the second of two mass graves of civilians butchered in Kosovo. NATO immediately became involved through extensive bombing of Serbian strongholds and transportation hubs and placed NATO boots on the ground to bring this genocide to an end. Kosovo marks one example of excellent response to unfolding genocide. It also marks one of the first major known instances where satellite imaging technology was used successfully for this purpose.

Postscript. I had always known that Ajsha was brilliant. Years after taking my classes and sharing her story, she and her sister graduated Harvard with their master's degrees. Today, they are off making the world a better place.

CHAPTER FOUR: D.R. CONGO (2002-2003): An Emergency Crisis Procedure at the CPG – A Massacre in Bunia.

"We have to control the city with 500 warriors just to observe; we have to be able to fire. We can't remain like that. If we are to settle the situation, the mandate must be changed."

Colonel Daniel Volo
UN Commander, forces in Bunia prior to mandate change that allowed force. 2003. [46]

Emergency Crisis Procedure at CPG on D.R. Congo – Bunia Massacre.

It was the end of a productive but uneventful summer at the CPG. We had great office space overlooking the Potomac River, 4,000 square feet of discounted office space as well as an indoor basketball court. We had funding woes, but the professional-looking office space helped us feel more secure. August 9th was the last day all of the interns would be at the

---

[46] http://www.guardian.co.uk/news/guardianfilms YouTube: Bunia Massacre – Democratic Republic of Congo

Center, so we decided we would throw a barbeque. We set up the grill on the penthouse balcony overlooking the river. At the lunch hour the interns handed in their country binders and headed out to the balcony. The stress of the daily work began to melt away. I had prepared thick burgers the night before and they sizzled with the hotdogs on the grill. The smell attracted everyone including the other offices. By 1:00pm the sun arrived, making it one of the most beautiful settings in Washington to say goodbye. Cory and a few others would stay until the end of the summer and of there would be our newly hired skeletal staff but the volunteer human rights monitors were the soul of the operation, and they were leaving. It had the feel of a seasonal hotel closing down for the winter.

I wiped my hands on my apron and added hotdogs to the grill. Cory gestured urgently to me through the window. Yevgeni, who had returned for his second summer, took over at the grill and I went in to see Cory. Her face was serious with worry.

"Rich, it may be nothing, but there's some trouble in Bunia, Congo."

"What's up?"
"Well, C has been emailing me frantically in the past few days and he just sent a note that seems pretty ominous. He's hinting that there may be a massacre occurring right now."

"Lendu on Hema?"

"No Hema on Lendu."

115

I looked at everyone outside relaxing and laughing. My mind went from the tranquil scene outside on the balcony to the flash of machetes and screams of terror in the Ituri Province jungle.

"When will you know?"

"Any minute."

"Okay, tell Roy to grab anyone involved in the emergency crisis procedure for DRC and give them a head's up, and to stop drinking."

She nodded then walked out. How ironic. The season is over. A day later and we would have only limited ability to react, but here it was at the last possible hour. The timing was uncanny. I took up my spatula, flipped a row of burgers and looked at the view of Washington. A helicopter flew low down the Potomac and passed close over the Key Bridge. They were getting closer and closer. One helicopter came so close to our balcony a few days before that it shook the structure and we all thought the tail blades would hit the side of the building. I looked back at the doorway. Cory was already walking back to me reading a printed email as she walked.

"It's happening. It's on. C is confirming a massacre on the ground in Bunia, Hema dialect speaking perpetrators with over a hundred dead and many wounded."

C was one of our best sources on the ground. We had met him when he had visited policy makers in Washington. He was biased, to be sure, but his information was always excellent. The only problem with C's information was that it would need independent confirmation before we could release it.

I looked at Cory:

"Okay, that's it. It's go-time. I want everybody on the emergency crisis team in the boardroom in two minutes. Let's go."

I went outside and handed my apron to Yevgeni. I cleared my throat. I addressed the group on the balcony.

"Well, Cory just received a first-hand ground report of a massacre unfolding in Bunia, Ituri Province, and DR Congo. This is not a drill. I need the five people on the emergency crisis team and everyone on the executive staff and the PR people to head to the boardroom. Now, the rest of you, try to be helpful to the DRC team after the meeting. Otherwise, finish your lunch. Jan take the grill."

The complexity of many ethnic and linguistic areas with a weak central government, a history of genocide and many well-armed militias, made D. R. Congo a constant threat to explode.

At the beginning of the summer, two months earlier, we had tried to get a grasp of the ground situation in DR Congo. It was a mess. We began to meticulously draw a map on our wall-sized blackboard to include each of the several rebel, foreign national armies and D R Congo government controlled areas. We counted at least 18 armed groups, some of whom had shifting loyalties. The list didn't even include the ethnicities like the Hema and the Lendu who were now battling in Ituri Province. Then, we wrote up the names of each of the groups and their alliances, modus operendi and strength. Now came the pivotal question:

"Which of these, are the bad guys?" I had asked.
Their answer, given in unison without hesitation, was jarring.
"ALL OF THEM."

This would be difficult. We divided the lists into different levels of massive human rights abuse. Those who were directly responsible for massacres were in the worst group. Those that *may* have committed massacres were next. Then we broke the civil war down into its several components. There was the Rwandan government involvement, the Ugandan presence, the RCD Goma proxy war, the Banyamelenge in the area, the Hutu genocidaires leftover from the Rwandan genocide of 1994, the Hema and Lendu militias, the rebel forces in the north, not to mention the several neighboring governments who had sent troops. Nine foreign governments had been heavily involved in the later stages of the DR Congo civil war, and at least fourteen militias were involved in the conflict being called the African World War. Most of these foreign forces had gone home during Joseph Kabila's first term. However, Rwanda and Uganda continued to keep forces there. On the surface, their reasons for being in D.R. Congo were well founded. Rwanda was still seeking the Hutu genocidaires who had fled to the Congo bush after the genocide. The genocidaires from Rwanda killed nearly 40,000 Tutsis living inside the Congo, Banyamelenge and in refugee camps. Uganda was asked to help keep the peace between the warring Hema and Lendu. Neither was exactly as it appeared. Suspiciously, Rwanda and Uganda both had record years of diamond and coltan exports during the time their troops were on the ground in DRC implying a taking of mineral resources that were not theirs. Rwanda also aligned itself with a rebel group called the RCD Goma who were accused of horrendous human rights abuse and employed this group in proxy warfare when it was convenient. Rwanda had agreed to remove troops and had resorted to tricks to keep some of their soldiers in DRC. One example of this was when Rwandan University students were marched from Rwanda to D.R. Congo at night and were marched back across the border to Rwanda in soldier's uniforms, under the eyes of the international observers. This was done briefly to meet the quota of Rwandan troops being withdrawn from D.R. Congo.

In the northeastern province of Ituri the feuding between the Hema and Lendu ethnicities destabilized the area. Uganda, originally asked by the UN to intervene for stability, ended up fueling the Hema and Lendu conflict to unrivalled proportions with the saturation of arms from Uganda. Suspiciously, Uganda's exports of diamonds and coltan also multiplied, raising the likelihood that they, too, were profiting off of the weakened state of the Congolese government. As long as the Hema and Lendu were fighting, Uganda could stay in order to provide stability to the area while benefiting from the Congolese resources. Uganda was asked to step in to keep the peace, twice.

The CPG staff looked at motivations, the ground situation, and dangers toward civilian populations until we had a clearer picture. We could not imagine a more complex civil war or human rights picture. Just a quick glance at the main player's acronyms was enough to make your head spin: UPC, RCD-ML, RCD-N, MLC, UPDF, RCD-K-ML, APC, RPF and the MONUC.

In brief, the government controlled the western region near the capital and far from the fighting. It had just made "peace" with one of the war lords in the north, Bemba, and had offered him the VP slot in the government, but unlike Caesar, when it came time to cross his Rubicon, he chose not to return to the capital but remained with his troops in the north – a Vice president on paper only. Years later he would run unsuccessfully for President against Joseph Kabila in a closely watched election. Many of the neighboring governments saw the benefit in supporting Joseph Kabila after the assassination of his father, the former communist guerilla Laurent Kabila. When Joseph Kabila assumed the reins of power, he was committed to a negotiated resolution to the civil war and diplomatically and effectively ushered the 'guest armies' to leave. It was in the East, where there were many armies and militias that the trouble always occurred.

On this day, August 9th, 2002, the day of the barbeque, a band of Hema militia had massacres a Lendu village. It appears that the massacre was a reprisal for an earlier Lendu attack on an unguarded Hema village. Our job was to obtain credible neutral third party confirmation. If we received the confirmation, we would need to get the information to whoever could stop the massacres. We would give the information to the press, but often times that did not have an effect. Even if the press published it, publication alone was not always enough to resolve a major human rights disaster. Our ultimate goal was to resolve the situation.

We closed the Board Room door.

The first step was formulating a strategy and assigning tasks to each person in the room and then agreeing on a second meeting in a short while. We decided to meet in a half an hour. Two people were tasked with drafting the press release. Two people checked the wire services and the regional and international media to see if word of the massacre was out. If the media already had news of the massacre, we could stop trying to get third party confirmation and could concentrate on releasing the information to the right policy makers. The rest of us worked on neutral third party confirmation. Cory and I, who were most familiar with the ground situation, divided the list of field contacts and relief organizations who had people in the area. It was 1:15pm when the meeting adjourned. By 1:45pm Cory and I were still working the phones. We changed the meeting time to 2:00pm.

At 2:00pm we all stepped into the boardroom. No one sat down. The press release first draft was read. It was rough and needed editing. The wire service and media search had produced nothing. It appeared no one was reporting this massacre. Again, we appeared to be among the first in the world outside of D.R. Congo to have the information. But we needed neutral third-party confirmation, and quickly. The UN staff in New York would start to drift toward their weekends in about two hours. It was crucial to get the information to the UNHCHR (now OHCHR) in New York because they were helping to draft the language for the new UN-flagged, French troops soon to be deployed to the area. I put John on the draft and everybody else starting hitting the phones with instructions if they got ahold of someone who could confirm the massacre, to get Cory and me immediately.

Around 2:30 Cory came into my office.

"Richard, call this number and ask for Jacques."

"Who is he?" I asked as I dialed the very long number.

"He is with the UNHCHR in Kinshasa."

I stopped. Good thinking. Smart. Who would know better than the UN High Commissioner for Human Rights Office in Kinshasa? Well, actually the UN presence in Bukavu would know better because they were within 300 miles of the massacre. But we couldn't get them on the phone because it was the middle of the night and the middle of a massacre. Even if we could get them on the phone, they would be very busy securing staff, protecting people, receiving and writing reports to send back to the UN. But the local office would certainly have called Kinshasa with the information so they could begin to file their report and request help as needed. But it was very possible that neither office had thought to call the UN offices in New York because they were swamped. That was where we could help.

"Ah qui?" Jacques hurriedly answered the phone.

"Bonjour, est-ce que Jacques?"

I introduced myself in my high school French. After one sentence of my French he broke into fluent English. I asked about the Bunia massacre.

"Yes, we heard about the massacre," he confirmed:

"Yes, at least 100 dead by the count right now."

"Jacques, we have information that the perpetrators were speaking a Hema dialect. Do you have that?"

"Yes, we also have other credible information that the perpetrators were Hema."

Now for the crucial question.

"Did you," I asked
"Pass the information on to UNHCHR in New York?"

"Mais non! Do you know how late it is here? There is too much to do. I have to go home and get some sleep to be any use tomorrow. I am going home." He sounded exhausted and said goodnight.

That was the confirmation we needed. We called another board room meeting. This was a strategy session to determine which agency was best suited to respond to the massacre.

Most of the four years at the Center were filled with research, editing, interviewing, developing contacts, phoning, emailing, writing, fundraising, and selling donated computers. Reacting to unfolding emergencies like the one in this story was rare. This was the time when all the preparation paid off with information that could save lives. For every one report the center published that had a tangible effect there were a half a dozen that achieved little except increasing awareness. But when our action did have an effect, I was always surprised at the timing of how close we would come to failing. Examples of this were; the phone cards running out just moments after we obtained the critical confirmation of the Sulawesi massacre; our asking the right bush pilots for information on Nuba just before USAID made some significant decisions regarding deliveries to the starving Nuba. A third coincidence was our fortunate timing as we called the UN offices in New York with the fresh confirmation from C and their *own Office* in Kinshasa.

After the phone call with the UNHCHR Kinshasa office we convened another brief meeting. We agreed that the UNHCHR was best positioned to help in light of the imminent troop deployment to the area. We called a UNHCHR contact in New York. After a series of transfers, I was required to have the same conversation with three highly placed officers inside the UN who were working on DR Congo.

"Hello Pierre, my name is Richard O'Brien. I am from the Center for the Prevention of Genocide. We are a nonpolitical, non-religious, nonprofit organization that serves as an early warning system for massacres worldwide. Our purpose is to bring breaking news of massacres to agencies and policy makers such as yourself. Pierre, the reason I am calling you today, as you may be aware by now, is that there has been a

124

massacre in Bunia just a couple of hours ago. Approximately 100 unarmed Lendu, mostly women and children, were massacred by a Hema militia. It is likely a reprisal attack for the recent Lendu on Hema massacre."

"Are you certain of your information, I mean, who are your sources?"

"Well I cannot reveal our primary source to you for reasons you can understand. However, our confirmation source is the UNHCHR Office in Kinshasa."

There was a pause at the other end of the line.

"Now why in the world would you have that information and we wouldn't?"

"Well, Pierre, they are writing up the report as the information is coming in. It is also in the middle of the night there so many of them have gone home. You know they probably have a few ground concerns as well."

"Who did you speak to in Kinshasa?"

"Jacques."

"How long ago?"

"Just a few minutes."

"You know the timing on this is extraordinary. Did you know that we are set to have an interdepartmental meeting about the level of the UN peacekeeping deployment and mandate recommendations for Ituri Province on Monday?"

"One of your colleagues had just mentioned it to me."

"That's quite extraordinary information, because, you know with an immediate threat that gives new importance to the numbers of peacekeepers and the strength of the mandate, their response ability."

"We thought the information could be used by your office." I offered.

"Can you send us the information you have?"

He gave me his fax and email and we sent the information off.

It really was amazing timing. If we had not taken the initiative, it is likely the exhausted Kinshasa UN office would not have had the time to submit the report to the New York UN office before the Monday meeting to determine the mandate language. When Pierre left the phone, they held a quick meeting at the UN regarding the breaking news in order to incorporate the information into the Monday meeting agenda.

In Monday meeting in New York, the UN raised their levels of peacekeepers in the area and included 'use of force' in the mandate language to protect innocent lives on the ground. This was language the UN peacekeeping force commander had requested for months. By having an early warning system in place, we helped make sure that the information, in a world where there is an overabundance of information, did not get lost in the noise or bureaucracy.

When trouble occurred in Ituri Province between the Hema and the Lendu and the Ugandans were in the process of pulling out due to international pressure, something unexpected happened on the UN Security Council. One of the Security Council members stepped up and took responsibility to stop the massacres. In Sierra Leone several years earlier, it had been the British, aided by some unusually effective mercenaries that had ended the massacres. But this time, unexpectedly, it was the French. Within one month of becoming fed up with international indifference to massacres in DR Congo, the French forces, under EU and UN auspices, arrived and halted the massacres in the Ituri and South Kivu Provinces.

While DR Congo has some of the most valuable resources of any nation in the world, today it remains fragmented and stymied by warfare and disease. The French force that went in, however briefly, showed again, that genocide can be combated by vigilance and action.

The stars sparkled under a clear Washington summer sky. The heat of the day had evaporated and a nice warm breeze passed over the penthouse balcony. Cory, Madoko. John, Yevgeni, Roy, Jan and I lounged on the outdoor chairs and took in the majesty of the view. Everyone was subdued. The significance of the events of the day was on everyone's minds. We fired up the grill and broke out the beer and at the end of the evening began to say our goodbyes.

CHAPTER FIVE: GUJARAT, INDIA (2002): INTERVENTION AND CONFESSIONS.

Confessions Caught on Tape. Bloodbath Averted by Sikh Police.

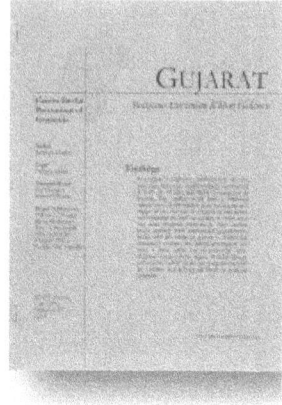

"We showed them what's what."

Babu Bajrangi, massacre participant bragging, Gujarat, India. [47]

On February 27th, 2002, a trainload of Hindu pilgrims, returning from a pilgrimage to sacred Ayodha, caught fire in the Godhra station and fifty-eight people perished in the blaze. The gruesome sight of the sheets covering the bodies, contorted in the shapes of the victims last desperate moments, enflamed the outrage of the majority Hindu population. A story immediately circulated about Muslims fire-bombing the train as revenge for an ongoing dispute between Muslim vendors who sold refreshments through the train windows and the Hindu pilgrimage passengers. Weeks later, the Indian government created a commission to investigate the fire. It found no credible evidence for this claim of Muslim responsibility. It defied logic that any person could climb into the cars, spread an incendiary,

---

[47] YouTube: Gujarat Massacre of Muslims Undercover Footage 1 of 3.

start the fire and escape unharmed and unnoticed. Nonetheless, radical Hindu nationalists produced lists of names and addresses of Muslims throughout Gujarat, distributed them to radical members and initiated large-scale killing. When it ended a few days later, more than 2,000 innocent Muslims had been murdered, including former Member of Parliament Ehsan Jafri. Parliamentarian Jafri had tried to intervene to stop the rape and killing of Muslim women and children in his apartment building. When he slipped money out of his narrowly opened door to the perpetrators, in an attempt to pay them to leave the innocents alone, the radical Hindu men pulled him outside and, in full view of his family watching from the balcony, hacked him to pieces. [48]

The tensions between the Hindu majority and Muslim minority dates back, in the modern age, to the separation of the newly independent Indian state into Muslim-majority Pakistan and Bangladesh (originally East Pakistan) and Hindu-majority India. The minorities of Hindus and Muslims remaining in these nations experienced the brunt of antagonism between these countries during times of tension.

Following the train fire at Godhra station, radical Hindus scoured communities looking for Muslims, some carrying lists of Muslims to target. The police stood aside as children, women and men were hacked to death and set on fire. Groups of radicals had their eyes on the Muslim minority, waiting for such an excuse to attack.

A few aspects to note on the Gujarat massacre and the government reaction make it unique. Not only was the violence unleashed not justified, but it was based completely on a

---

[48] Ibid., Video 1.

misinformation – an assumption that the train caught fire because of a Muslim bomb. This first disaster compounded into one of geometrically larger proportions. The government reaction to prevent further massacres was praiseworthy and effective. It is also unique because several perpetrators were caught on film bragging about their exploits in murder.

Confessions Caught on Tape.

An industrious journalist went undercover to infiltrate the Hindu national groups that perpetrated the massacres. Once he was accepted as part of their group, he inquired about their roles in the Gujarat Muslim massacre. Surprisingly, several of the leaders and perpetrators proudly told him of their roles in the killing spree. Their new recruit carried a very small video camera which recorded through a buttonhole in his shirt or a tiny hole in a book he held. Caught on camera were 'confessions' of these average men who took extraordinary measures to kill innocent Muslims. One radical Hindu killer described the plan: "What happened was, the people we've had in our sight for the past twenty, twenty-five years, we selectively killed those people." Another describes their plan to kill the Muslims as a 'Hindu Jihad.'[49]

Babu Bajrangi appeared to be the most talkative of the perpetrators as he gleefully described the horror he perpetrated, as if it were a sports game. "There was this pregnant woman, I slit her open. We showed them what's what."[50]

---

[49] Ibid., video 1.
[50] Ibid., video 2.

130

Most police stood aside as the killing occurred. One victim, Fatima, described the police response when she asked for help for her family. "They said (the police) 'we have not been ordered to spare your lives. Our orders are to kill you'"[51] Almost all of Fatima's family died.

This type of journalism, facilitated by the improvements in technology, helps make the world a more transparent place. The prosecution of these men was slow, yet after years of delay, this stark video evidence was used to prosecute a portion of these perpetrators. The unfiltered view into the minds of perpetrators is eye-opening. Evil is present in the human heart everywhere, in every continent and in every nation.

Bloodbath Averted by Sikh Police.

While heroism is always praiseworthy in these circumstances, the most effective way to combat the next instance of genocide or mass atrocities is prevention. Early warning and education are cornerstones of that prevention. It is interesting to note the different reactions between authoritarian governments, which usually do not act to prevent these types of abuse, with the responses of democracies, when confronted with internal massacres or genocide. India, the world's most populous democracy, attempted to grapple for a solution to help prevent future reoccurrences of violence in Gujarat. While the two activities they undertook did not receive much press attention – they were, nonetheless, very effective in preventing continued massacres of the Muslim minority. First, they

---

[51] Ibid., video 1.

published a report which concluded that Muslim vendors were *not* responsible for the fire. This helped reduce tension. The danger remained, however, that in large public celebrations, especially religious celebrations, misunderstandings and tempers could flare, or lists could be maliciously distributed again and massacres reignited. The government of India chose to be proactive. They hired several hundred Sikh police officers, as Sikh's were neutral in this conflict, to show a strong presence at all public events and celebrations. Those Sikh officers acted as a buffer between these groups, helping to prevent tensions from flaring into violence. They succeeded, as the police presence diffused the situation. This is a classic conflict-prevention strategy. It was not front page news but it is likely that it saved lives and allowed a nation to move forward.

CHAPTER SIX: UGANDA
L.R.A CHILD-MILITIA
MASSACRE ACHOLI.
A Ugandan Boy.
Alice and the Spirit of an Italian
Soldier. Testifying Against the LRA

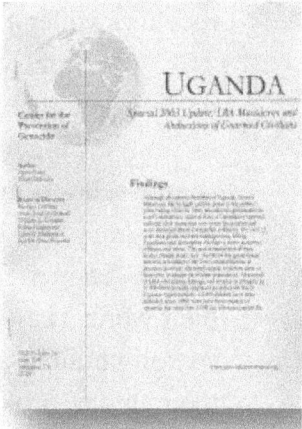

"They looked for students who wore
our shirts and killed them. They
reversed years of work in hours.
They're gone."

> Aid worker in Northern Uganda
> after massacre of their students
> by the LRA.

A Ugandan Boy.

The LRA militia, mostly teenagers, came into town on horseback, in vehicles and by foot. Many of the boy's family fled and were cut down in their tracks. Others tried to hide and were discovered. Many were raped before they were butchered. The dead bodies were stripped of valuables. He hid, then fled to another burned out hut and then to some bushes. The militia caught him near the edge of the village, beat him with rifle butts and left him for dead. He woke in pain when they were gone. His eye was swollen shut. He began wandering for days. His feet, face and arms swelled with infection and disease. He survived on plants and collapsed on the roadside miles outside of a protected camp where he was discovered near death. After a while he could stand and talk a little. He was six years old. To me, his swollen face is the face of genocide.

The photo of the little boy who was almost beaten to death was the most poignant thing I had ever seen. It came to us from a Christian aid group in the area that helped build and supply schools for the Acholi. Three British nationals from the relief group that had provided the photo, met us to discuss the region. They were charming people who were serious about their work. They told us how despite their hard work to provide Acholi children a safe haven, the LRA had swept into one of their camps, seeking any of the children wearing the camp tee shirts and killing many of them. It had disheartened even the most diehard relief workers from their organization.

Alice and the Spirit of an Italian Soldier.

The LRA is the militia the Lord's Resistance Army, a cult militia that used children to fight while they operated in northern Uganda. The movement started in 1985 when Alice Lakwena (Auma), was struck by an illness and emerged claiming she had been taken over by a spirit of a dead World War One Italian Captain who was infused with Christ's spirit reborn. Many other spirits shared her body and she convened meetings with these spirits in the wilderness.[52] She developed a following among some of supporters of deposed President Okello and declared war on the government. Her group armed itself with hymns, Shea-nut oil and strode into battle against

---

[52] *The Economist*, Obituary 1/25/2007

Ugandan government troops in 1986-7. The frightened government soldiers fled the battlefield from this hymn singing display. Ultimately, a government artillery barrage in the summer of 1987 showed the thinness of Alice's spiritual

Author
Diana M. DeGroot

Editorial Staff
Richard O'Brien
Amen Schaefer

Board of Directors
Richard O'Brien
Amb. John McDonald
John C. Heidenrich
William A. Douglas
Barar Ferdinand

1921 N. Lynn St
12th Floor
Arlington, Va 22209
Phone: (703) 528-1082
Fax: (703) 528-5776
info@unionovertheworld.org
www.genocideprevention.org

UGANDA
Country Report Update

Large-Scale Massacres in Northern Uganda:
LRA-Perpetrated Violence Escalates

Center for the Prevention of Genocide
Winter 2004

CPG Publication.

protection as the Holy Spiritual Movement warriors were killed and dispersed on the battlefield. Alice fled by bicycle and said the spirits had left her. She spent most of the rest of her fifty years in the Dadaab refugee camp. But a fragment of her militia continued under the leadership of Joseph Kony, who claimed to be her cousin. Kony declared himself to be filled with the same

Holy Spirit as Alice.[53] The newly named LRA (Lord's Resistance Army) claimed to be fighting to install a government ruled by the Ten Commandments. Kony and the LRA proceeded to break almost all of them, especially 'thou shalt not kill.' From a seemingly non-violent cult movement under Lakwena (Auma), the LRA transformed into one of the most viciously cruel child militias on the continent.

In 1987, Joseph Kony began a guerilla warfare campaign against the government using child soldiers to attack local Acholi villagers in northern Uganda. The campaign targeted local Acholi villages, travelers, clergy, schools and anyone that had food or money. They raped, abducted children and killed many villagers. Their primary goals were their own survival and to instill terror and their chosen method was to live off of the belongings of the villages they massacred. The children they abducted were forced to kill other children to prove their loyalty to the LRA. A boy, asked who in the crowd was his friend, would hesitatingly point to a friend. A pistol with a single bullet would be placed in the young boy's hand, 'kill your friend,' he would be told. When he hesitated, the militia would threaten, 'kill your friend or we will kill you.' Either the boy would comply and be bonded to the other LRA boys in a bond of shame and murder, or he would be killed and the LRA would continue the gruesome initiation with another young boy.

At the height and through the end of the LRA presence in northern Uganda, thousands, then tens of thousands of women and children walked dozens of miles every night to the relative safety of the government-protected camps. They were

---

[53] Ibid.

fleeing the LRA violence that often came at night. They would walk back to their unprotected villages in the early morning hours. This was a man-made migration to preserve life. It is almost as strange an activity as the child cult-militia it was fleeing from.

Testifying Against the LRA.

The longstanding President of Uganda, Yoweri Museveni, attempted to disarm and defeat the LRA several times, the most notable effort being 'Operation Iron Fist.' The porous Sudanese border, however, and a complicit al Bashir Sudanese government gave the LRA a safe haven. Eventually, Sudan closed its borders to Kony's militia and the Ugandan government was faced with the unpleasant challenge to disarm or kill abducted child soldiers, in order to protect the innocent. To get out of this Catch 22 situation, Museveni chose a controversial course of action; he let them leave Uganda. He offered Kony safe passage to D.R. Congo with the promise he and his militia would be unharmed as long as Kony pledged to never return to Uganda. When Kony and the remnants of the LRA fled to eastern D.R. Congo, they brought their madness with them and have been directly responsible for several large-scale massacres in D.R Congo since their arrival. Recently the LRA has also been active in the Central African Republic as that nation plunges into civil war, mass atrocities and chaos, largely unrelated to the LRA presence. While there now exists a large reward for the capture of Kony, and the U.S has forces tracking him, one cannot help but wonder whether the best opportunity to capture him was when Museveni willingly let Kony slip through his hands years earlier.

The Center for the Prevention of Genocide (CPG) published four full reports on the LRA massacres in the area. Our first report came out in 2001, and then one in each of the following years. Because places existed where people were dying in greater number, Uganda was always overshadowed. In the other countries tens of thousands were dying or were in danger: Nuba, Sudan, Sulawesi, Indonesia, Ituri Province, D.R. Congo, Darfur, Sudan In Uganda, the LRA massacres would stop for months at a time, the LRA would disappear, then begin again when they reappeared. Unlike other places that had garnered international front page attention, the numbers of victims in Uganda were in the dozens, not the hundreds or thousands. It was more difficult to get anyone to notice an area with no strategic importance, no lobby power, a low grade war and a low grade genocide. However for the Acholi people living there, it was pure hell.

Early in 2004, we lobbied Congress and the Africa Sub-Committee to take more action regarding the LRA. We found that most of the offices clearly needed a tutorial. Uganda's LRA was a group with which most lawmakers and staffs were unfamiliar. The CPG worked with the Africa Sub-Committee to appear with Acholi local leaders, flown in by Human Rights Watch, to inform the Congressional Africa Sub-Committee of the LRA terror. We provided detailed testimony in Congressional staff briefings. But it was not enough. Over a decade later, the LRA continues to function in the bush of central Africa today.

The author testifying in U.S. Congressional Sub-Committee hearing on the massacre of Acholi by LRA in Uganda, March, 2004.

Catholic Church Ocheo
P.O. Box 678
Soroti - Uganda
16/8/2003

Dear Joanne,
        greeting
from Ocheo. How are you? For
us things are very bad. The
rebels are burning houses, killing
people, burning food stores and
abducting children between the
ages of 8 - 18. Things are very
bad, people are on the run
for safety. Ocheo Shops, mission
School are just full of refugees
who have no food, clothing and
shelter. It's a real disaster.
    Lwala mission was looted,
priests beaten and 3 million
shilling stolen. Then they went
to Lwala girls S.S.S and

abducted about 70 girls. Some
have escaped after being raped
many time, some are not yet
back. The situation is bad.
    Now the 2nd wave have come
to reinforce the 1st group and
they are much worse, killing
anybody they come across, not
Sealaus and the soldiers just
fear them. The road to Soroti
is blocked and Soroti - Katakwi too.
Things are bad and no help
to these suffering. So Ocheo Parish
under mission has organised some
food help to these refugees here
and some used clothes, but
they just can't meet the enormous
needs of these suffering people.
    Pray for us here.
            thanks
                Fr. Lawrence
                    Ocheo

139

Letter of firsthand atrocities committed by the LRA – referred to as rebels.

CHAPTER SEVEN: NUBA, SUDAN: INTERNS EXPOSE MAN_MADE FAMINE.

"Where the hell did you people come from? We can't get any information out of Nuba."

Roger Winters, US AID

Interns Help Prevent a Man-Made Famine Against Nuba.

Joanna and Yevgeni, two new interns, were assigned to research and make contacts in the South of Sudan and to follow up on reports of massacres, human rights violation, ethnic cleansing and slavery. Many human rights organizations had been monitoring South Sudan for years. Militias hired by the Sudanese government had ethnically cleansed, massacred, starved, raped and enslaved the Nuer and the Dinka among other ethnicities of the South. The abuse was a continuation of the jihad which had led to the civil war and an effort to depopulate the oil concession areas that the government had sold to foreign corporations. Until the Comprehensive Peace Accord of 2005 was signed, slavery was actively practiced and entire regions had been depopulated by Baggara militias hired by the government. It was perhaps the most likely place where we might find genocide occurring. Our pair of interns emailed, phoned and laid out maps to track activities in the region. They approached human rights NGOs, aid groups and UN agencies to get a better understanding of the ground situation. After a week of research they approached me with an unusual revelation.

"Rich, we want to ask if we can change the scope of the area we are working on?"

Yevgeni started. Joanna continued. "We think that there are a lot of human rights organizations concentrating on the South of Sudan and the information is pretty much getting out to the press and policy makers. But we wanted to take a closer look at an area in the Central part of Sudan, the Nuba Mountain range."

"Why, what's going on there?"

"Well, we're not sure yet. But there is a government ban on travel there so there are very few relief organizations except for small ones that don't worry about the danger to themselves and are mostly Christian based. But the thing is, it seems that the government is bombing the relief as it comes in, so that the Nuba will starve and have to leave."

"Bombing them, really? Are there oil field in the area like in the South?"

"No, that's the strange part. This area seems not to be so strategically important. But we'd like to ask your permission to change our focus, contact people there, the relief organizations, and the bush pilots, to get a better picture of what's happening there."

"Okay but know your stuff before you hit the phones. Know your towns and questions. You can try the Colonel next door, he may know some pilots in the area."

"Thanks Rich."

They left my office with beaming smiles. That was to change two days later.

Joanna and Yevgeni came back to see me, two days later in the afternoon. They looked miserable. They had contacted a number of the relief organizations on the ground to no avail: wrong numbers, disconnected lines, no answer and messages left unreturned, but then they turned their attention to the bush pilots. Their first call was a disaster. On the same floor as the CPG in the white building on the corner of King Street and Payne Street in Old Town Alexandria, there was a Colonel who flew aid missions to Central America. We believed our gruff neighbor was a CIA operative. Yevgeni and Joanna wondered if he knew any bush pilots currently flying into Sudan. He did. The Colonel met with them late the previous day and gave them contact numbers of a friend of his who flew relief flights in and out of the Central areas of Sudan. In their excitement to contact the pilot, they mismanaged the call. Having woken up very early that morning to take account of the time difference, they made the call with a phone card for Africa. They successfully got through to the pilot but, in the course of the conversation with the tough, no-nonsense military vet, they forgot to lay out a map out and got some names of towns confused, and instead asked about massacres and relief work that was occurring several hundred miles away. Their inexperience and lack of preparation was apparent. He told them off and hung up. Not quite the reaction they expected from a pilot doing what they considered to be noble work.

"You don't even know where El Obeid is? What the hell are you doing wasting my time? What organization is this? Make sure you don't call me again."

The pilot's criticism was tough. They felt sufficiently bad that I tried to encourage them.

"Okay, good. What did you learn?" I asked.

"Not to get on the phone until we're really prepared."

"Right, well that's fair enough. You two are off the phones until you are tested to make sure you're ready. This is a good lesson. It's the real world. Brush yourselves off, go get a bite and then do your research. Learn what you need to know to speak authoritatively on the area, read the UN reports, look on the internet, find out what the ex-pat Nuba community is saying then come back to me."
"Okay."

143

They looked devastated. I continued.

"Look, we're flying blind here. We're all trying to do something that we've never done before and maybe no one has. We're going to make mistakes. But the only way you're going to make a difference and help these people is if you suck it up, work harder and learn from your mistakes. Don't take it so hard but also don't put yourself and the Center in that position again."

They smiled at the prospect of actually getting out of the Center for lunch as well as the chance to redeem themselves. And so it became policy, that before reaching out to contacts, every human rights violation monitors who worked in our office had to take a quiz and do a presentation to an executive staff member before contacting sources or policymakers by phone, email or in person.

A few days later, Joanna and Yevgeni presented marvelously, were quizzed flawlessly and were back on the phones calling everyone and anyone on the ground they could contact. They developed a good lead with some of the bush pilots. These pilots were those who would fly the aid into the Nuba Mountain area in spite of the government ban on travel. However, these pilots had never heard of us and they were wary that the Sudanese government was setting them up. Joanna and Yevgeni felt that some confidence-building measures were in order. They asked if we could help the pilots in some way in order to earn their trust. They felt the pilots could become an invaluable source of information. Time would prove Yevgeni and Joanna right.

They asked the pilots what we could give them that would help them in their job of delivering aid to the Nuba. The answer was startlingly clear: they wanted Cold War-era maps of the area. During the cold war both the US and the Soviet Union produced maps of the area that still remain the best and most accurate since the end of the Cold War. Recently, cheaper and less accurate maps had proliferated the market. The good maps were no longer easily found, increasing the danger for the pilots. The government did not hesitate to target these planes that brought the aid, because they were in violation of the no-travel ban. Often the maps would be inaccurate by several miles and would lead to needless flying or force additional approaches to the landing strip, all of which subjected the pilots to extended time as targets for the artillery.

Joanna and Yevgeni, along with four other volunteers went to the US Archives and the Library of Congress, to find the maps. We purchased hundreds of dollars' worth of maps. They were huge: two of them covered an entire wall in the boardroom. We sent these to Nairobi where most of the pilots originated. Within days the pilots received the high quality maps, and we began receiving some of the best information anyone could get out of the area.

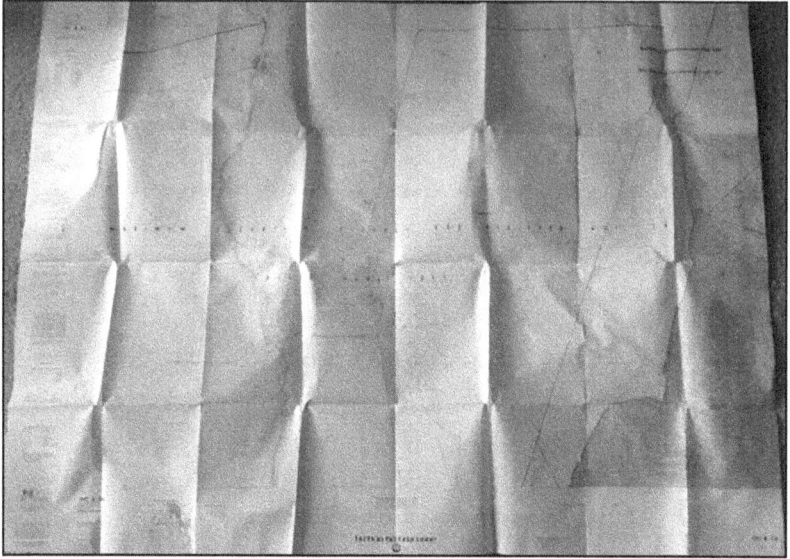

Photos of wall-sized map sent to Nuba relief pilots.

The first piece of information we needed was 'why.' The narrative we told to policymakers must be accurate, compelling and make sense. The question of, 'why would the government care enough to bomb the Nuba?' was one we would have to answer. The pilots felt that there were two reasons; first, that the oil pipelines passed through the area and, second, because the Nuba Mountains was a place where moderate Muslims lived peaceably with the Christians and animists. The radical regime in Khartoum wanted to rid Sudan of its Christians and depopulate the oil regions to give them easy access to the concessions they were selling to foreign companies. As a peaceful region of moderation, the government saw the Nuba area as a threat to their radical religious agenda. In order to depopulate the area, the government began sending planes into Nuba to bomb the fields during planting season and attack the farmers with machine gun fire. An area that had been self-sufficient for most of its recorded history was now without crops and the relief couldn't get through because of the travel ban. So the diehard smaller Christian charities like Samaritan's Purse, Christian Solidarity Worldwide (and International) and others would fly illegally into the area, land and unload quickly and get out. In any case the government would target any planes before, after or as they unloaded.

The information began to come to us daily. When the pilots returned to Nairobi at night, they would send us an email outlining how many people had been killed in the most recent bombings. They even included how many cows and chickens were killed and wounded. One report read:

"No fatalities but four cows dead, three injured, fourteen chickens dead, and eight injured."

We thought reporting on the number of chickens injured or killed was strange. Later it became apparent that these figures were important because it strengthened the case for man-induced famine that we were to make at USAID.

Within weeks we had enough thorough evidence of a man-induced famine that was sponsored by the government of Sudan. We began the process of writing the report. While the government was not massacring the Nuba, nor sending them to gas chambers, the willful blockading and purposeful bombing of the civilian food supply fit clearly under the Genocide Convention. Article 2, Section C "bringing about conditions in order to destroy a race, religious, ethnic or national group." It would be a while before the full report would be written, edited, re-written and printed, so I asked Yevgeni, Joanna and others to compile an advanced report for presentation at USAID.

A nutritional analysis based on ground information had predicted that 30,000 Nuba would perish within months, even weeks, if 2400 to 3000 metric tons of aid didn't reach the Nuba. The rainy season was approaching and if the aid wasn't delivered before then many would perish. Urgency was crucial.

As the staff worked on the advanced report, the US was taking an increased interest in Sudan, thanks to the efforts of many human rights and relief organizations, as well as indigenous groups. One such person was Jemera Rone of Human Rights Watch who had consistently gathered and released massive amounts of information each day from the region. She monitored all goings on in Sudan like a watchful, concerned and protective mother. She worked hard and ceaselessly as one personally charged with the protection of the victims of Sudan. Eventually her information, combined with the work of scores of organizations, had brought the plight of the Southern Sudanese to attention of the US policy makers. The result: former Senator Danforth, accompanied by USAID Director Natsios, went to Sudan on a widely reported fact-finding mission. The government of Sudan, however, denied them access to the Nuba Mountain area, under the guise of protecting them from the dangers in the area. One of the parties was able to make a brief landing at one of the stable government-approved sites where there was no violence. By the time the US delegation left, USAID and the State Department were very concerned about conditions in Nuba.

The Center made the appointment with USAID at this critical moment when they sought legitimate information on Nuba. Roger Winters, one the most influential Africa specialists at USAID, sat across the table from me and as I ended my presentation said:

"Where the hell did you guys come from?" Before continuing.

"We can't get a thing out of Nuba and you've got the bombings down to the cows and chickens!"

We explained we had canvassed the small religious based relief organizations in the field as well as the bush pilots who flew in their aid and he was satisfied.

Our meeting was in a basement USAID office without frills. It was Winters and one aid. Our papers that outlined the first-hand accounts of the abuse were spread across the table. The premise of the meeting was that the Center for the Prevention of Genocide was about to make its first determination of genocidal conduct. It would be in the Nuba Mountain Range of Sudan and it would be a man-induced famine. The findings, I added, would also highlight the likelihood that USAID was one of only a few organization that could pull off the rescue in time. We covered the information one more time and went through the integrity of the informational sources without compromising their identities. We ended with a specific request for USAID to undertake strategies to deliver the 3,000 metric tons of sorghum to the area. When we finished, he looked like a man on a mission.

One week later USAID officially requested the Sudanese government lift the travel ban to the Nuba Mountain range for the expressed purpose of avoiding the man-induced famine. One week later, with permission in hand, under Natsios's supervision, USAID began delivering the 3,000 metric tons of Sorghum to the Nuba and staved off starvation for 84,500.

* * *

Over the next several months we were to meet with and become familiar with many of the Nuba leadership in exile in the US. They helped provide pinpoints for massive human rights violations in the area. While we couldn't use their information without independent neutral confirmation, they proved to be invaluable in knowing where to look. Some of the Nuba wives would bring in a tomato and peanut-paste eggplant dish that I still remember fondly.

Akila was the tallest Nuba with a charming smile and a gentle way. He was 6'7' and had to duck when he entered and exited doorways. He had briefly played at the top level in college basketball until injuries sidelined him. One evening he stopped by my office to say hello. As he sat his unfolding legs took up most of the free space in my office. We talked about our families. He was regretful that he could not go home and help his grandfather before he died. For Akila, it was impossible to get there. As a known Nuba leader, the danger of returning to the Mountains was severe at the time. I asked what his grandfather died of. His grandfather, he told me, had died of starvation. I was shocked. There was no one left of the family in the village. No one to take care of him. They found him dead and alone in his dwelling. He had been too weak to go to town during the government man-induced famine. There had been nothing Akila could do about it a half a world away.

The USAID had saved 85,000 Nuba. Approximately 500 Nuba starved. That number did not seem high until Akila said his grandfather was among them.

CHAPTER EIGHT: DARFUR, SUDAN (2003–2004)
Lists of the Dead.
The Credible I.C.C Threat and Sudan's Hitler.

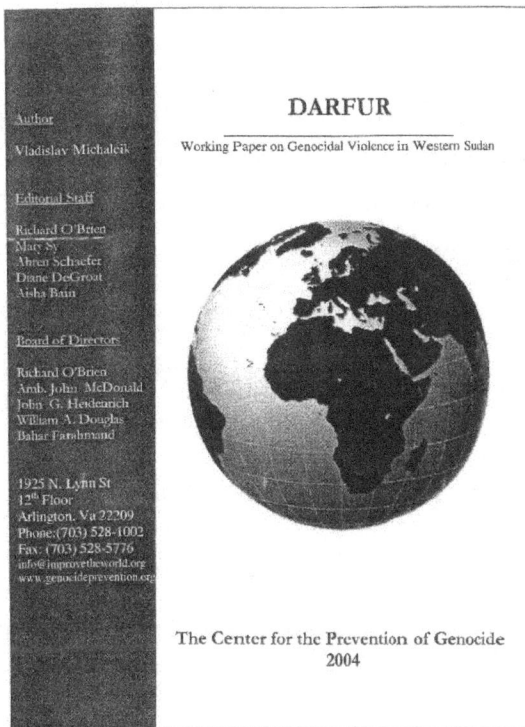

DARFUR

Working Paper on Genocidal Violence in Western Sudan

Author

Vladislav Michalcik

Editorial Staff

Richard O'Brien
Mary Sy
Ahren Schaefer
Diane DeGroat
Aisha Bain

Board of Directors

Richard O'Brien
Amb. John McDonald
John G. Heidenrich
William A. Douglas
Bahar Farahmand

1925 N. Lynn St
12th Floor
Arlington, Va 22209
Phone:(703) 528-1002
Fax: (703) 528-5776
info@improvetheworld.org
www.genocideprevention.org

The Center for the Prevention of Genocide
2004

"In the time we have been here today, more women and children will die violently in the Darfur region than in Iraq, Afghanistan, Palestine, Israel or Lebanon. So, you won't need the UN – you will simply need men with shovels and bleached white linen and headstones."

George Clooney, American Actor, Activist

151

Lists of the Dead.

The lists came to us late in 2003. They were handwritten names of boys and men who were all dead. We were asked by the Nuba leadership to meet with a group of Darfurians who wanted to share urgent information about government abuse in Darfur. We met with them in the board room of the CPG and they unfolded the lists of the dead in front of us. We spread them out and studied them. After a few minutes I asked the delegation if we could be excused for a few minutes. My executive staff and I went to my office.

"What strikes you about these lists? What do you notice?" I asked.

"They're all Muslim names" one responded,

"They're all men." another added.

"That's it. What else? Look carefully."

They looked for a few seconds until someone pointed out the ages.

"That's right. These are all men and boys between 16 – 62 years of age. These could be considered fighting-age males. There are no female names among several pages of the dead. So, what happened? That's what we need to know. What's the context, the story here? Were the men and women separated and only the men executed? Was this a pitched battle and these are the names of the dead? Are there any neutral third parties in the area that can

152

confirm the context of these deaths? These are questions we need to ask."

We returned to the meeting room and explained our dilemma. We needed context and neutral third-party confirmation before we could publish. The list could be the dead from a civil war or rebel clash. The man who provided the list explained that he had simply received the list from his cousin who had said these were the names of the dead in the village they were from, and that the government had killed

them. This explanation brought up another issue. He was the second or third hand source. We would be the third or fourth hand source, without confirmation or context. I knew immediately we could not publish the list. While we resisted red tape preventing us from doing our jobs effectively, there still needed to be certain ground rules for confirmation of the information. Otherwise, it was likely that we would report incorrect information and hurt our credibility. Credibility was crucial with policymakers.

"Can you go back to your cousin and get the context of what is happening. What was the story? How did these people die? Also, are there any aid groups, humanitarian, human rights or any other neutral groups that may be in the area that we can reach to confirm this information?"

CPG Compilation of Confirmed Massacres in Darfur, Sudan

The Center for the Prevention of Genocide has monitored conditions in Darfur since the summer of 2003. On January 20, 2004, eleven elderly people perished in a massacre, which occurred in villages north and south of Kuttum. In addition to the massacres, numerous incidents of looting, rape, torture, and abduction have been reported. Unfortunately, the travel ban on the region has made neutral third party confirmation extraordinarily difficult to obtain.

Date: February 10, 2004
Location: Shatatya
Victims: 81 civilians killed during an attack on Shatatya and surrounding villages

Date: January 20, 2004
Location: Various villages to the north and south of Kuttum
Victims: 11 elderly civilians killed and 24 villages destroyed in *Janjaweed* raids

Civilians Killed:
1. Mohammed Adam Kahleel
2. Issa Abakar Khaleel
3. Abdulaziz Mohammed Noor
4. Yousid Mohammed Jummah
5. Tiganie Ahmed Yagoub
6. Mohammed Abdulmajeed
7. Ismael Yahya
8. Yousif Abdullah
9. Maryam Ishag
10. Khadeeja Yagoub Mohammed
11. Khadeeja Ahmed

Villages Destroyed:
1. Jakhana
2. Tarainga
3. Loobous
4. Naro
5. Boon
6. Taraigna
7. Amoo
8. Bargna

Lists with actual names given to CPG of the dead by genocide in Darfur, Sudan.

He was pretty sure there was nothing but Darfurians there, but he would ask. We explained why we couldn't move forward with the report until we could get confirmation. There was a possibility that we could move forward if we had significant detail of the context, and so declare it an unconfirmed report. After all, if Jewish escapees from the concentration camps during World War Two were the only people who could verify the existence of gas chambers at the time, one would not expect Nazi, or third party confirmation. In fact Rudolph Vrba and Alfred Wetzler, who actually did escape Auschwitz and tried to tell the world about the gas chambers, ran into this exact difficulty – without third-party confirmation, their story was questioned.

Over the course of the next two months, more lists came to us with increasing amounts of information, including occupations and towns the dead were from. Eventually stories and context came with the lists.

"Early in the morning Janjaweed horsemen came into our village and began burning our grain supplies, killing men where they found them and raping the women who had not fled. The men were unarmed…"

The stories took on familiar patterns, with the government providing helicopter cover fire while these deadly Arab horsemen conducted policies of ethnic cleansing, rape and what appeared to be, genocide.

A combination of events made us decide to declare the situation genocide in early 2004. In our working paper on genocide, we concluded that the preponderance of evidence made a strong case for the government of Sudan's complicity in genocide in Darfur. The Board of Directors knew that the CPG would probably close its doors when we lost our leased/donated space at the end of April. We were in debt, had no working capital, and the prospect of losing our space meant we could no longer fulfill our mission. With this knowledge, we made the decision that it was better to call Darfur what all evidence indicated it was: genocide, rather than waiting with the information for independent confirmation while innocent people continued to die. The massacres and ethnic cleansing in Darfur needed to be published and word of the genocide needed to be put into the mainstream media. While I spoke out on national public radio about Darfur during those weeks, more needed to happen.

***

During the last board meeting there was a lot to cover over and the mood was very somber. The only bright news was that I was finally able to push four names through for the CPG Humanitarian Awards. With no resistance, it passed. We would give out our human rights award. There were several individuals who had sacrificed much and had accomplished an incredible amount of life saving, genocide preventing work. For years I had wanted to acknowledge them. Now we had a chance to do that, and to help Darfur's cause and to do one last thing. It was the ten year anniversary of the genocide in Rwanda: it was time to remember their loss as well.

The four individuals were quite unique and spanned the political spectrum but were similar in one very important way. Each had moved mountains to save lives that, had it not been for their effort, would have been lost. The Reverend Steven Snyder was one of the individuals who directed the 'help us were being massacred' email to us, regarding the slaughter in

157

Sulawesi. (See Introduction chapter) We had approached him when we were compiling our Moluccas Report and he shared information freely. He had provided photographs to be used in a national PBS special on genocide (Genocide Factor) for the section on Indonesia. His mission was both religious and humanitarian, and he was passionate about both. The reverend selflessly ministered to Indonesians in danger, provided aid as well as human rights reports that had proven instrumental in stopping massacres in Sulawesi and elsewhere. His altruism had cost him his life. He had died of kidney failure after becoming ill while in Indonesia.

Andrew Natsios, our second choice, had to cancel the receipt of his award as he flew across the globe to respond to an emergency. Natsios, as the head of USAID, had on several occasions lead the charge or even put himself in physical or professional peril to fulfill USAID's mission. He authorized the aid for the starving Nuba in Sudan during the man-induced famine in 2001. He personally had nudged both the US and the Sudanese government to make this happen. When North Korea teetered on the brink of another man-induced famine, he worked to make ensure there was no repeat famine and wrote an authoritative book on the subject. There are a host of countries and ethnicities that owe a debt of thanks to Natsios's efforts though he is rarely mentioned in the press. He helped bring attention to the plight of the Darfurians in western Sudan, even placing himself in danger when a riot broke out at one of the refugee camps. He placed himself in the way of an angry mob that wanted to kill a government spokesman. While he probably understood the crowd's anger toward the official who had threatened the already displaced crowd, his appreciation for life made him naturally step into the breach to stop the killing.

When others might have been reluctant to overburden the work, he pushed forward to assure massive aid reached those in need. He represents what is best about US foreign policy.

The last two awarded are human rights icons. The calm and laid back John Prendergast had worked in the Clinton administration before establishing himself in the ICG concentrating his efforts on D.R. Congo and Sudan as well as the Great Lakes region. Unpretentious, straightforward, with long hair and a sometimes shaved face, John could break down a question or explain a complicated situation in the simplest and easiest of terms. Sometimes he would just shrug and say something casual like 'you got me on that one, I'm not sure, maybe one of the other panelists would like to tackle that one. His business was human rights and his casual appearance belied his seriousness of purpose. He deserved to be acknowledged not for his cool demeanor but for his timely information and fact finding throughout the region. He lived and slept in these conflicts, knew most of the nuances and was, in my estimation, the second most influential NGO person in the United States regarding the eastern region of Africa, where so much of our work was concentrated.

Finally, Jemera Rone. I knew her name long before I met her. Day in and day out we would receive reports about the most detailed human rights abuse in the South of Sudan. It was easy to receive 4-10 emails a day from her listserv. Her information was excellent, her sources outstanding, and her timing, impeccable. I sincerely believe that had she not been born, the 17 year civil war in Sudan, with its slavery, massacres, ethnic cleansing, rape, torture and man-induced famine, would still be going on today. Many of us wouldn't have known where to look for information. When Jemera smelled smoke, you

159

could be sure there was a human rights fire going on in Sudan. We wanted to acknowledge the work of Prendergast and Rone in human rights, but we also had a hidden agenda. We wanted the Darfurian community to link up with these two human rights specialists on Sudan. When I presented her the CPG Humanitarian Award I said:

> "Like a Chinese water torture, drip by drip, she constantly reminded the international community and policy makers about the horrors in Sudan until they broke down and paid attention to it."

Her tenacity saves lives. Though she hated it, she should be applauded and upheld to the next generation as a model, a challenge to the saying 'you cannot possibly make a difference.' In places as hopeless as Sudan, remember Jemera Rone.

We decided to hold one final big event that would encompass several ideas. It was the ten year remembrance of the Rwandan genocide: we would walk with a candlelight procession from the American University to the Rwandan Embassy, where the Rwandan Ambassador would greet us and give a speech. Before the walk, at American University, we would have an awards ceremony for the four award recipients. This event would be a rare opportunity to help the struggling Darfurian community, who needed word of the genocide they faced to reach the right hands. It was a success on each of these levels. After securing the march route permit from the American University to the Rwandan Embassy, we confirmed the Rwandan Ambassador as a speaker. We created the award plaques and invited many communities. But we especially targeted the Darfurian community in exile.

The award ceremony was flawless. The speeches were touching. The Reverend's widow steeped her statement with Christian references. Jemera and John spoke well and were honored. As the ceremony broke and we began to form up for the candlelight walk, three and a half miles to the Rwandan Embassy, the Darfurian leadership crowded around the podium.

They had come from Arkansas, California, Canada, Florida and elsewhere across the US with the sole purpose of bringing attention to the plight of their people. They had driven, taken buses and flown to get here. They crowded in to thank me for the invitation and the work we had done, but this was not the time for it.

"Guys, listen. This is a big opportunity for you. There are two of the biggest forces in the US for human rights, specifically regarding Sudan. They are standing there holding plaques that tell the world that they are the best at this. This is the time to meet them, make appointments, tell them the stories of your family members being killed and figure out how you can coordinate your activities with them."

"Jemera!" I called out. She came over as did John Prendergast, and introductions were made all around and the buzz began.

"The next time you folks are coming to town we should definitely put some time together to meet and coordinate events." The words just came naturally out of her mouth.

"That's part of the problem Jemera, they are scattered and it's difficult for them to organize as spread out as they are. But, as you can see, they are willing to get their message out policy makers on the hill and elsewhere, they'll show up in full force."

The Darfurians and Jemera and John did the rest of the talking. Numbers were exchanged, appointments were made and over the next months as I moved to Florida, I read report after report that stemmed from the American Darfurian community, through Jemera and John. Within three months Congress used the term genocide to describe the situation in Darfur as well as the US Secretary of State.

I felt that Darfur was finally getting the attention it deserved when during the presidential debate both George W. Bush and John Kerry called the situation in Darfur by its proper name – genocide. I let out a battle cry whoop during the debate when I heard it. John, Skee and several others who had worked at the Center, separated by thousands of miles from each other, let out similar battle cries of satisfaction, long after the Center had closed its doors.

The Credible I.C.C Threat and Sudan's Hitler.

Postscript on Darfur. In the nine years since I wrote the first part of this chapter, Darfur worsened with three million of its people internally displaced within Sudan and externally in neighboring Chad. Hundreds of thousands remain displaced today. The massacres, burning of villages and ethnic cleansing slowed down in 2009 but the fallout was enormous. Sudan remains devastated through displacement and hardship and the perpetual fear of further government repression. Significantly, it was not the dozen of human rights organizations, nor was it the policy makers, politicians or even the 9,000 person African Union force, that ended the genocide in Darfur. It was the I.C.C When the International Criminal Court handed down its indictment of Omar al-Bashir for crimes against humanity and then genocide, it was impactful. Even though Bashir said he would kick out the aid organizations, as punishment for the ICC indictment, he relented. Omar al Bashir did what was unthinkable only a few years before: he allowed the southern part of Sudan to have its referendum on independence. When South Sudan voted overwhelmingly for independent, al Bashir, unbelievably, let it go. The split happened and South Sudan became independent. A reason why this was relatively easy for al Bashir was that much of the oil concessions had already been sold to foreign companies and the treaty did not challenge that ownership. Finally, al Bashir scaled down and eventually stopped the scorched earth policy for Darfur.

When I think of Omar al-Bashir, I think of Hitler. This man is evil. But even evil men try to protect their own skin. I firmly believe that the I.C.C indictment and the resulting travel

163

restrictions that accompany it were instrumental in ending the genocide in Sudan. It irks me that he is still in power there. But the lesson here is that a single piece of paper, backed up with the force of international law and potential consequences can prove to be a very powerful tool against even the most evil of powerful men.

The crowd of 400 begin to gather at American University for the C.P.G Awards Ceremony and Darfur/Rwanda March. Next Page: The author, Jemera Rone, Widow Snyder and John Prendergast of ICG, and below, Jemera speaking with the Darfurian leadership. At least 100 Darfurian leaders and their families were present from across North America. The leadership met Rone and Prendergast after the ceremony.

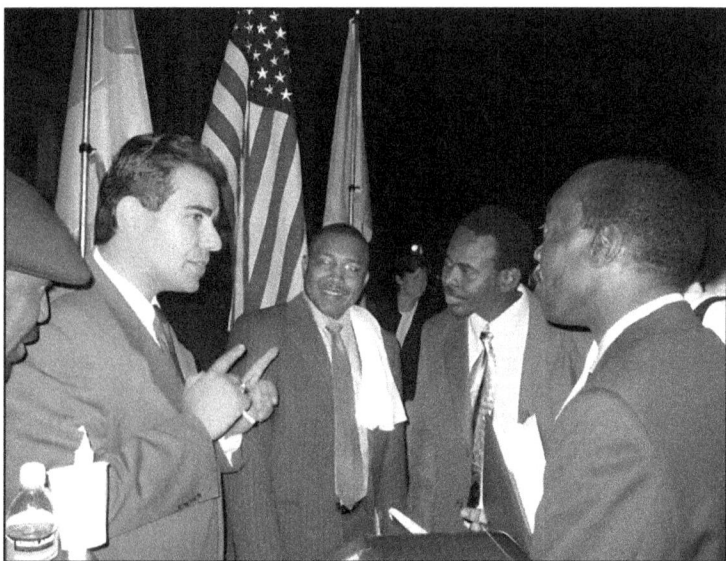

The author encouraging the Darfurian leadership to advocate to Jemera Rone and John Predergast during the march.

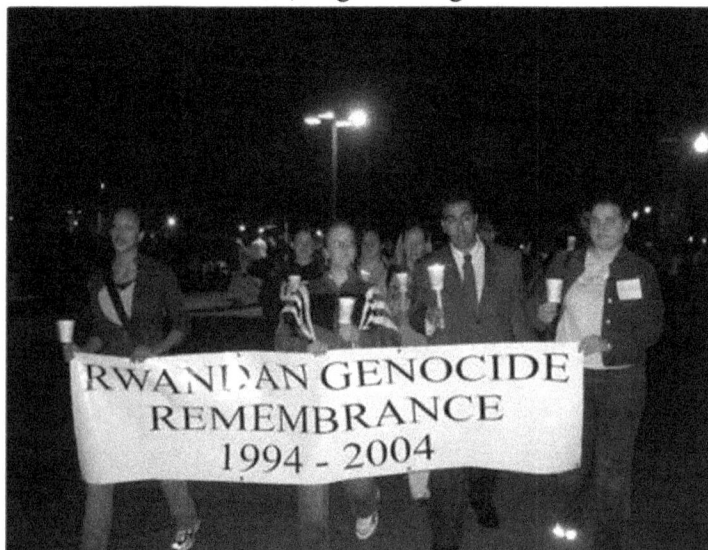

Hundreds marched from A.U. in DC to the Rwandan Embassy on the remembrance of the Rwandan genocide and also to bring attention to Darfur, Sudan.

CHAPTER NINE: THE CENTER FOR THE PREVENTION OF GENOCIDE: STORIES OF A STUDENT-LED EARLY WARNING SYSTEM.

Sergio Vieira De Mello Lay Dying.
"Help Me, Help You."
India-Pakistan Nuclear Non-Proliferation Report
Chechen Refugee Camps

CPG staff in October of 2001. Next page, CPG staffs and interns, 2002 – 2004.

Sergio Vieira de Mello Lay Dying.

Laying underneath tons of rubble, whispering his last words to his wife 'I love you, hurry back' was the end of the life of Sergio Veira de Mello.

His wife frantically ran from soldiers to administrators trying to get their attention to focus on digging Sergio out from under the ruble. You can see her doing this on the films of the aftermath of the bombing. His death is symbolic of the failure of the UN and the world community to properly gauge the needs when responding to world dangers, whether genocide, warfare, terrorism or even natural disasters. Sergio's death was due to an al Qaida bomb, but it was also due to the ineptitude of the rescue mission. When they finally lifted the body of the dead hero out of the rubble, unbelievably the two UN flags that adorned his office were draped underneath him.[54] He died on a bed of UN flags.

A few hours before he had felt a sense of relief to pack his belongings and prepare to return to his position as High Commissioner for Human Rights at the United Nations in Geneva and then back to his native Brazil for a brief visit with his family.

De Mello had been hand-picked to help oversee the writing of the new Iraqi government's Constitution. The position would, on the surface, be a step backward or, at best, laterally, for his career, but de Mello did not hesitate to go where he could do the most good. There were already rumors that he was an emerging favorite pick for the UN Secretary

---

[54] *Sergio*: One *Man's Fight to Save the World*. Introduction. Samantha Power, Penguin Books, 2008.

General position. The Constitutional Assembly was difficult to manage and the tempers ran very hot on several issues. But in the end, they finally drafted a document that enshrined individual rights, the rule of law and protection of minorities – and put that power in the hands of a people who had never known this right or power.

The al Qaida-built bomb destroyed part of the compound and took the man's life but did not undo the work of a lifetime. De Mello died, but the Iraqi Constitution lived.

Eight months before this, I met Human Rights High Commissioner de Mello for only a few minutes on his first day on the job. That chance meeting lead to our little-known CPG reports being read and considered at the highest levels of the United Nation. He was a class act in his bearing and his life's missions had an effect on millions. His name should be remembered and life's mission should be continued.

"Help me, Help You."

I arrived at the UNHCHR headquarters, showed my ID at the security booth and waited inside. As I was escorted upstairs, I noticed the hushed tones and politeness. It struck me as a very civil place, not overly stuffy, but a building maintained with class. Everyone's behavior was impeccable but personable. Allison LesBlanc met me at the office door.

"Mr. O'Brien, so good of you to come."

We sat across her desk in her small office and I thought,

'This is the desk where the problems that plague the humanity of Sudan come.'

It wasn't quite as simple as that, but she certainly was one of the people you would want to reach if your Sudanese cousin was in danger.

I asked if she would mind if I presented for ten minutes about the Center's work, the reason why I was in Geneva, and what I would like from her. She agreed. I began by telling her about the Center's purpose, that it was created to anticipate massacres and was often among the first organizations in the world to obtain information of impending or unfolding massacres. I told her about our rigorous standards, how we confirmed with neutral third party sources, reached out before the trouble began so we would have a working relationship with people on the ground. I told her of the inroads we had made with policymakers in order for them to take us seriously. It was important for her to note that we were not religiously or politically aligned, and that we responded with urgency to all major human rights violations that had an aspect of genocide to it.

I explained that before the beginning of each new college semester season we go through an extensive hiring phase where we review the resumes and interview the top candidates who apply to serve as Human Rights Violation Monitors. We identify the areas where genocidal conduct is most likely to occur, looking primarily at factors that include recent history, predisposition to massacres and the presence of any trigger mechanisms. Trigger mechanisms can be any one of a number of actions: ranging from an assassination of a crucial leader, an election, a food shortage, or the forecast of reprisal massacres. Then, we assign one, two or three volunteers to each 'hot spot.' They learn the history, the key players and the indicators of likely trouble that may occur. They reach out to established contacts on the ground to introduce themselves, and they create links with new contacts to get better real-time information out of the country. They monitor their area and watch for danger signs. If nothing happens, good, they can work or their secondary country or aid with the editing of a report. But if something does occur - a trigger to a massacre, a militia surrounding an unarmed town, relief deliveries being restricted so that man-induced starvation ensues - if anything like that occurs, the volunteer has to be ready to work with the executive staff in the emergency crisis procedure. That procedure includes confirming the incident with a known neutral third party, or finding an independent, credible and neutral source to confirm it. The next challenge is getting the information into the hands of those who are in a position to stop the massacres. We had developed extensive contact lists of people in-the-field for each country we monitored, as well as comprehensive lists, phone numbers, faxes and email for every policy maker in each agency, government or national body that could possibly affect a positive outcome for the area. We also kept extensive local, regional, national and international press lists and cultivated relationships with journalists in the areas we were looking both as sources for us and to enlist to publish our breaking news. (See the Appendices for examples) The key to our success, as a small operation, was planning ahead of the emergency crisis to build relationships with people who could help resolve the situation.

Some of the contacts would come from unusual and unexpected sources. We found one in a bar in Nairobi. We were given the number of a reporter from an internationally respected media outlet, with a satellite phone. This particular reporter had not been getting published as much as he thought he would like and felt neglected. He had excellent, thorough information, and he had risked his life to gain it, yet it was hardly being published. We could understand his predicament; he was sitting on a treasure trove of information but was unable to convince the editors back home of the pertinence to the home readership of a D.R. Congolese guerilla war. We found him, over the phone, as he sat in a bar in Nairobi. He was willing to talk and had excellent information on the ground situation. His help pointed us in the right direction of Bukavu just before it exploded.

The second part of my presentation to Allison LesBlanc was to recount our actions in the Nuba Mountain range, our work getting the information to USAID and their subsequent reaction. This was her area of expertise. I concluded with a summary of the hotspots we were presently working on and the likely aspects of genocide in those conflicts. She looked impressed. We discussed Sudan for a few minutes and ways we could collaborate in the future on mutually confirming human rights violation information. Then she looked at me askance,

"Who else do you have appointments to see?"

"No one."

"No one? Why not? You really should see John at D.R. Congo, Allyssa at Uganda, Boris at Chechnya, Claude at Burundi."

"Yes, I know. The trip was very last minute and Geneva wasn't even on the agenda until I had your appointment. I think it would be a great idea to get together with each of them to see how we could collaborate. But that depends on one thing."

"What is that?" she asked,

"You." She looked at me for a few moments, and I continued,

"If you can commit some time, let's say fifteen minutes on the phone, sometime today, to just pick up the phone and call ten of your colleagues for a minute each. Be my scheduler for fifteen minutes. I'm at your disposal, as many meetings as you can schedule, whenever, late this afternoon and tomorrow. It would be an indispensable service and I honestly believe it is true to say, no one else can do it for me but you."

I paused, let her think, then I asked:

"Can you help set that up?"

She looked again at me and smiled.

"You picked a great time for it. I have a meeting literally in a couple of minutes. But, hmmm."

She seemed to be going over her tight schedule in her mind.

"Okay, right after that meeting I will get on the phone and see if I can set something up for today and certainly a few meetings for tomorrow. But give me a little time."

It was 3:30 when she called back.

"Okay Richard, if you are still available, I have set you up for four brief appointments today and two tomorrow. The appointments today are at 4:00, 4:15, 4:30 and 4:45 at the following desks, Uganda, Chechnya, D.R. Congo and Burundi."

She gave me the names and advised me to get to the security booth soon so I could make all the meetings and then instructed me to come by her office at 5:00pm for details of the next day's meetings. I hung up impressed. Whoever thought that the UN was just an ineffective bureaucracy should have experienced her efficiency.

The first meeting was with the stern faced Allyssa regarding Uganda. She actually produced our Uganda report out of her top desk drawer, and said it was the most thorough report of massacres in Uganda she had seen to date. We discussed channels of information and, as we spoke, I noted the universal sadness in her tone and expression. I realized her sense of despair was well grounded not only because of the massacres in Northern Uganda, but also because she was responsible for five other countries in the area – an unfathomable amount of human rights violations for one individual to police effectively. I understood why her eyes were so heavy.

The next meeting was conducted entirely in French with the desk officer for DR Congo. Surprised at myself for agreeing to conduct the meeting in French, I squeezed my brain hard for the right words or close approximations and turns of phrases to express my points and the purpose of the visit. When I couldn't remember the words, I would rattle off a sentence in English and Jean was comfortable with that. He had a warm personality and detailed knowledge of the complexities of the ground situation in DR Congo. It was fortunate that my needs were simple to communicate. I needed two things. First, contacts at UN agencies on the ground in DR Congo and, second, his assurance that if we passed him breaking news, he would pass it up the chain of command at the UN. He instantly agreed to both and began jotting down the number of a contact who was on the ground near the massacres in the lawless eastern regions of DR Congo. (See Chapter Ten – D.R. Congo – Bunia Massacre). We parted with a genuine amiable grasp of each other's forearms and a half embrace.

The last scheduled meeting that afternoon was with Boris, a Bulgarian responsible for monitoring the Caucuses. He was amiable and collaborative. We agreed that the most pressing danger to unarmed civilians in Chechnya was the impending liquidation of the Chechen refugee camps in Ingushetia. At the end of our meeting he asked me if I would be attending the reception that evening for Sergio Vieira de Mello. I couldn't believe my luck. De Mello was recently appointed to direct the UNHCHR (OHCHR today) and could probably be counted among the top three people at the time to influence human rights endeavor in the world. I naturally agreed to attend the reception.

After the last meeting I returned to Allison's office.

"So, you wrangled an invitation to tonight's event, did you?"

"Actually, Boris was kind enough to invite me."

"Well that was another thing I was going to talk to you about."

Boris arrived at the door and we made our way to the reception downstairs.

Sergio Vieira de Mello was arriving today and the reception was his introduction to his Geneva UNHCHR staff. De Mello was a well-liked and well-travelled Brazilian diplomat. He was tall, distinguished and youthful looking. He had impressed U.S. President G.W Bush despite political differences. His reputation as a fearless trouble shooter helped place him as High Commissioner for Human Rights at the UN. Less than a year later, in a magnanimous act of courage, de Mello temporarily stepped down as High Commissioner for Human Rights, a safe and influential job in Geneva, and assumed another UN mission in Iraq. He was placed at the head of the UN's effort to oversee the creation of a legitimate Iraqi interim government and constitution. De Mello went to Baghdad, oversaw the creation of a respectable interim government and a well drafted constitution. Before he packed his bags to return to his High Commissioner position in Geneva, a van loaded with a massive bomb detonated right beneath his window at the Canal Hotel. The bomb ripped through his building and trapped him under tons of concrete. He lived for few hours as he lay pinned by the enormous immovable weight. There the refined gentleman died alone, after bidding his wife return with help. The soldiers at the scene could not or would not listen to De Mello's wife's pleas to help him. She and his surviving staff tried digging him out of the rubble with their hands with no success.

I walked into the open area, crowded with about 75 UNHCHR staff. Eight months before the bombing, he was alive and well and surrounded by well-wishers who vied for his attention and favor. I turned my attention to the buffet of food that was spread out along three tables, and the good wine that flowed easily. I made a point of limiting my wine intake to a glass and a half. It would be good to be a little relaxed. As I looked around the room and was introduced, I found that I was the only non-UN person present. At one point I saw Bernard from Burundi light up as he saw an old friend and fellow Burundian from across the room. As they approached each other slowly and smiling, the two old men neither shook hands nor embraced, nor did they kiss cheeks. They smiled and then slowly and affectionately lowered their heads and touched foreheads in one of the simplest, most graceful greetings I've ever seen. They smiled and laughed as old friends.

I watched de Mello and was surprised by two things; first, he had a polished, rich cadence in his voice. He exuded wealth and elegance. He held his mouth down around the corners and spoke with what appeared to me to be an aristocratic clipped tone. The second surprise was that he seemed supremely bored or perhaps just tired. He appeared to give the person introducing themselves about ten to fifteen seconds to engage him before his eyes would glaze over and he

178

would occupy himself looking elsewhere in the room, occasionally saying, "Oh, yes, yes, yes, yes," "I see, quite interesting, yes-yes." It seemed like he wished to will himself out of the situation.

I needed a good hook to catch and keep his attention. Years of teaching high school and the book *How to get your Point Across in 30 seconds or Less* by Milo Frank had taught me the value of getting your subject's attention right from the start. I thought for a while then decided on the memorable lines from the movie *Jerry McGuire*. In the movie, the main character is a sports agent whose career has taken a bad turn and his only client is a surly, but talented, football receiver whose attitude is preventing both of them from making the big pay day. The film is known for many famous lines including *'show me the money,' 'You had me at hello'* and *'Help me, help you.'* I knew which one was perfect for this occasion. I waited a long time until there was a lull in the conversation. De Mello had just informed the crowd that his door was always open and that any new, fresh ideas about how the UNHCHR could work better he would be interested to hear them. Despite giving a meaningful pause, it seemed that everyone there was intimidated to make a suggestion of any kind and to risk their relative anonymity and security. Perhaps they just didn't want to show off. But I took the cue and said:

"Early warning systems are a great way to save thousands of lives and millions of dollars and almost no one uses them."

I stuck my hand into his and introduced myself to him. By the time I said my name and the name of the CPG, his eyes were already moving on. They had glazed over and he was already gazing off into the distance. So, in a familiar way, I put my other hand around his elbow; he wasn't going anywhere. I asked;

"Do you remember the movie, *Jerry McGuire?*"

He stopped the progress of his eyes away from me and came back to regard me.

"Yes. I remember the movie."

"What was the famous quote from that movie? There were many of them, you remember? One was 'you had me at hello,' but the most famous one. Do you remember it?" I asked him.

"Ah, yes, yes, oh what was it." The schoolboy, brightest kid in the class machinery was spinning, working trying to retrieve the long ago stored information. I offered a hint:
"Show, me…the?

"Ah, yes-yes, I know this, yes SHOW ME THE *MONEY!*" He said loudly, like the character in the movie.
"That's right! Good job!" He looked pleased.

"Now, Commissioner, there were many good quotes in that movie. Do you remember when Tom Cruise's character, the sport's agent, was talking to his hardheaded football player in the locker room? He finally gets frustrated and what does he say to the football player. De Mello looked puzzled, so I gave him another hint:

'Help, me…help…"

De Mello's face was searching his memory, he knew it.

"Oh, yes-yes, HELP ME, HELP *YOU*!"

"You've got it!" I encouraged. I paused and waited for his attention.

"Well, that's why I'm here."

I said and stopped short. He looked at me mystified.

"I am sure I don't know what you mean, but I am interested."

He seemed genuinely puzzled and intrigued and smiled.

"High Commissioner, I run an early warning system that watches for genocide and massacres. Often times we know of massacres well before the rest of the world. What a monumental shame it would be if we had information that your staff was in danger, or their charges were in danger, and we couldn't navigate your chain of command quickly enough to get the warning into the right hands. So, 'help me, help you.'"

"Oh." He paused and thought this over for a moment.

"Hmmm, 'help me, help you'. Ah, that's terrific. I quite see it now. Brilliant."

He smiled at the simplicity of it, then said the magic words:

"Have you met Bertie Ramcharam, yet?"

I hadn't and I had been hoping to. Ramcharam was number two under De Mello and was the glue which was pivotal to the smooth operation of the UNHCHR. Knowing him meant potential access to the top UN Human Rights agency. De Mello led me by my elbow to his office manager, who arranged the appointment with Bertie Ramcharam for the next morning.

Milo O. Frank's *How to Get Your Point Across in 30 Seconds or Less* had shown me how to strike effectively in business, politics, human rights, job interviews and personally, when time was limited. But it was Mark McCormack's *What They Don't Teach You in Harvard Business School* that taught me when to say 'no' in business, how to observe and listen 'aggressively' and when to leave after you have achieved your goal. Satisfied, I smiled, finished my drink and returned to the hotel.

As I waited in Bertie Ramcharam's office I surveyed Lake Geneva from his office. The CPG had a great view of the Potomac River, but somehow his view seemed more majestic, more significant, more fitting for an influential UN office. Ramcharam was professional and vastly intelligent. He made the persuasive case that while the Geneva contacts would be no doubt good for collaboration; the best contacts for effective results for the CPG were the UNHCHR (now OHCHR) at the UN in New York. By virtue of their proximity to the most powerful people in the General Assembly and staff, the UNHCHR in New York had more influence and the ability to get things done. He provided me with a list of names of desk officers and regional supervisors to meet with when I returned to the States. I could use his name to open doors.

On the way back to the States, I stopped in Reykjavik, Iceland. Despite missing the auroras borealis and their famous puffins, I could not stop smiling. I was amazed and kept thinking: 'the UN will work with us!'

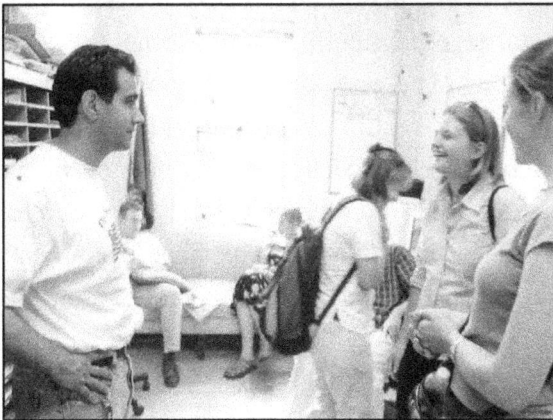

CPG interns at Mishas Café, office at King/Payne, Alexandria, VA.

India-Pakistan Nuclear Non-Proliferation Report.

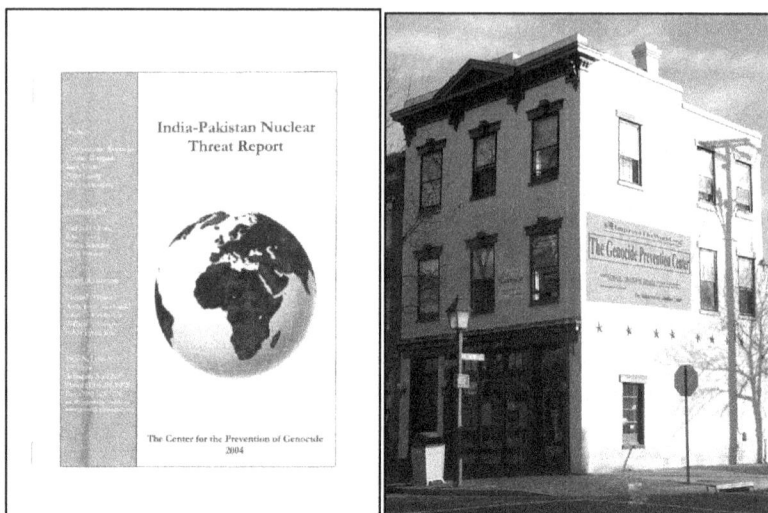

The C.P.G India-Pakistan Nuclear Threat Report and the original C.P.G HQ on the corner of King St and Payne St in Olde Towne, Alexandria, VA 2000 – 2002.

I remember Chris Forster's first day at the CPG, clearly, because it started out embarrassingly for me. I was alone in my corner office with no one due for an hour. I was alternately checking my email, reading my paper and spinning in my chair over to the other desk to check wire reports and press. My desktop had the radio on with Madonna's 'Celebrate' playing. The music had just brought me to my feet when the celebration was interrupted by a voice and a cough.

"Ah-hem." In a British tone.

"Ah, Rich"

It was Skee and behind him was a distinguished looking gentleman. The Brit behind him, Chris, coughed and looked away uneasy.

"Yes?"

I tried to sound in charge as Madonna blared in the background.

"I'd like to introduce Chris Forster. Chris, Richard, Richard, Chris."

"Oh, yes, Cambridge, right?"

"No, Oxford, actually." He looked blandly at me.
"Great, well Chris, you are a little earlier than we expected so why don't you have a cup of coffee, look at the paper and I'll sit down with you in a bit?"

"Ah, right."

"Skee, would you show Chris to the coffee, the newspapers and the board room."

"Sure Rich."

I gestured for Skee to come back afterward. When he returned, I pulled him in close.

"Skee, do you know why we come back and tell a person that they have a visitor first before bringing them back?"

"I think I now know why."

"Because they could be dancing, badly, to Madonna and fall immeasurably in the eyes of a future employee."

"Not to mention mine." He smiled.

I finished reviewing a report, put on a professional demeanor and went to the board room. Orientation with Chris took 45 minutes before we headed back to my office to discuss his schedule.

During the whole meeting Chris was very rigid, almost unfriendly. He answered questions stiffly with a minimum of syllables and I foresaw difficult times ahead if this was his manner of communication. Previous experience told me to discuss the communication differences right away.

> "You know Chris, it's good that you approach the work seriously, it is serious work. However, the work is so serious that we try to lighten things up around here when we're not in a crisis. The workplace culture here is much more laid back than I imagine you are used to in London. I want you to feel free to be yourself, let your personality come through while being respectful of others."

He looked somewhat confused for a second.

"I see." He said.

"Your serious demeanor is right and correct for the work, but just be yourself with the staff. They're a good bunch, easy to get along with."

"Mr. O'Brien, back at Oxford," he deadpanned,

"I was the life of the party,"

His face looked straight ahead and then a slight smile crept across his face.

I laughed. You could immediately tell that he had a good sense of humor and would fit in. And he did. By the end of the summer he had helped produce one high quality report and laid the groundwork for the India and Pakistan report, one of our best reports ever. He also pitched in and helped move hundreds of computers the CPG sold to stay open, played some basketball and made some good friends.

It was at the time Chris was compiling sources for our India and Pakistan Nuclear report that our website was hacked. We did not even realize that a hacker had intruded. Apparently, some hackers like to crack the site and just look around. According to our technologically skilled neighbors, this particular hacker was about fourteen years old and lived in London. One of their technology company employees was Mo. Chris had asked Mo to take a look at some technical problems and server issues we were having and, as a good neighbor, he did so without charging. A little later on in the day Mo came back laughing to us.

"Well I fixed your server, you had a routing problem where signals were bouncing back and forth because of your wiring and hubs."

"In English?" Chris asked.

"I fixed your server problem?"

"Ah, right, good man." A relaxed Chris smiled.

"But there was another issue that took a little more effort and finesse."

After he told Chris the story, Chris brought Mo back to my office and he told the executive staff.

"Well, you had a hacker. Nothing serious just someone looking around, a kid actually, fourteen years old."

"Fourteen!"

"Yeah, well, it's pretty easy stuff. So I researched him and got his address and emailed him that I was the authorities and that if he didn't cease and desist this type of activity, we would send a squad car over to him from Scotland Yard."

"That's priceless, how did you get his address?"

"Trade secret. Anyway, he tells me he doesn't believe me. So I asked him if he had a fax machine and he says yes and gives me the fax number. When I send him this fax he gets back online and he's crying, begging me not to tell his parents, promising he'll never do it again."

"What was in the fax?" Someone asked.

"Do I want to know" I added.

He flipped a piece of paper he was holding over to show a detailed satellite image map with a large Ferris wheel in it. The kid's house was circled. When the kid saw the satellite image of his house, he immediately thought that Mo was the authorities and shut his intrusion down immediately.

Chris Forster was the lead on our India-Pakistan Report. Unlike the Gujarat Report that concentrated on massacres of Muslims by Hindus in India, this report stepped outside of the CPG traditional reporting areas. During our research into the near war between India and Pakistan in 2002, a report quoting Pakistani dictator Musharraf leapt off the page. He indicated that when the Indians had amassed their troops on the Pakistani border in response to the bombing of the Indian Parliament (by terrorists who had links to the Pakistani government), that Musharraf had decided if India were to invade to use 'non-conventional' weapons. Pakistan is not known to have ever possessed chemical weapons and so the assumption is he was speaking about his willingness to use the dozen or so nuclear warheads Pakistan possessed against India.

While this was not genocide in the strictest sense, we found it difficult to justify away the potential threat to hundreds

189

of thousands and potentially millions of unarmed civilians on both sides of the border. The more we looked into it, the more disturbing the reports were. India and Pakistan have no 'hotline' for communications like the US and the USSR had during much of the Cold War. They shared no military protocol for escalation and de-escalation like the US and the USSR, so when the passions are running high, there is a realistic possibility of unbridled escalation without proper protocols to slow and check the military atavism. Lastly, there were no confidence-building measures in place which could undermine the distrust between the two nations. Essentially each nation had first strike capability, with massive destructive results for each country. But with less than three minutes response time between launch and arrival of missiles, in some cases, narrowed the capability for containment or the ability to pull back on a false alarm. A nuclear confrontation could happen, quite easily, by accident. And there would be no time, no mechanism and no trust in the information to put the genie back in the bottle.

We realized that we were not qualified to write the report because we had no nuclear non-proliferation, analysis or safety experts on staff. We looked for an expert who could write the report and attract top experts in the field to do the same for the price of lunch. We found him. Congressman Kopetski was a forty-something, youthful, recently retired member of the US House who had led the recent effort to ratify the START II Treaty. Because his retirement was not voluntary (he lost his re-election) he had time on his hands and agreed to meet us for lunch. After two hours of interns and staff entreating him to come on board and help write and attract specialists, he relented. The sushi lunch was his only compensation with the notable exception being the success of the report he and Chris Forster helped create.

Chris facilitated Kopetski's outreach to nuclear non-proliferation experts. Within three months the report was finished and available for placement at the first India-Pakistan governmental meeting since the near war of 2002. We managed for the report and a letter paper clipped onto it to be in front of every participant at the conference. The general in charge of the conference allowed it. The report showed the projected number of Indians and Pakistanis who would die in the short and long term during several accidental and intentional nuclear warhead detonations. It spelled out clearly in the report and the letter the heightened risk present without military protocol, 'hotline' communications and confidence-building measures.

When the participants left, newspapers reported that they agreed on nothing, nothing except that the next meeting should include on the agenda – military protocol, a communications 'hotline' and confidence-building measures regarding nuclear protocols. These were covered in the June 2004 conference between India and Pakistan. The Institute for Defense Studies and Analysis recognized in the pictured report that the areas our report emphasized were discussed and worked on between the two nations, perhaps because of our nudging.

February 12, 2004

Peace Conference Attendees,

The Center for the Prevention of Genocide is presenting the attached Nuclear Threat Report authored by leading non-proliferation experts in the hope to elevate efforts to address the issue of nuclear tensions between India and Pakistan.

The Center encourages participants to consider several important issues highlighted in the report. These concerns include the significant risk of nuclear conflict between India and Pakistan, given the lack of established nuclear protocol. The report further demonstrates the catastrophic implications for the populations of both countries if nuclear weapons are employed.

Finally, in the interest of preserving future peace, the Center calls on the representatives of both India and Pakistan to place a high priority on continued communication to establish a future agenda that includes risk reduction, the development of nuclear protocol, and confidence building measures. Such measures are imperative in promoting a stable and peaceful future.

Regards,

Ahren Schaefer
Fellow

The India-Pakistan cover letter attached to the report was featured on the negotiations table for each participant.

From the Institute for Defense Studies and Analysis

Nuclear Confidence Building Measures (June 19- 20, 2004)

The June talks on nuclear confidence building measures (CBMs) dealt with measures to 'reduce risks relevant to nuclear issues'.

Hotlines

Some old CBMs were given a facelift and some new ones agreed upon. For instance, the two sides agreed to 'upgrade', the 'dedicated' and 'secure' hotline between the Director Generals of Military Operations (DGMOs). It was also agreed that one more line between the Foreign Secretaries should be established. Thus, there would be three hotlines, 'upgraded', 'dedicated', and 'secure' for handling crises. If the two sides are still not able to establish a connection, the fault may not lie in the cables but in other exchanges in New Delhi and Islamabad.

1999 Lahore Agreement Re-Invigorated

The Lahore Declaration was followed by a Memorandum of Understanding (MoU) signed by the two Foreign Secretaries (K. Raghunath and Shamshad Ahmed). It reiterates the determination of both the countries in implementing the Simla Agreement in letter and spirit. It encompasses the gamut of issues which are now being pursued and calls upon the two sides to undertake "bilateral consultations on security concepts and nuclear doctrines, with a view to developing measures for confidence building in the nuclear and conventional fields, aimed at avoidance of conflict". It also calls for the two sides to "provide each other with advance notification in respect of ballistic missile flight tests"; "undertake national measures to reduce the risks of accidental or unauthorized use of nuclear weapons"; "abide by the respective unilateral moratorium on further nuclear tests"; and "periodically review the implementation of existing CBMs", including links between the respective Director Generals, Military Operations.

Nuclear CBMs

On the nuclear issue, the two sides have reaffirmed their 'unilateral moratorium' on conducting further nuclear tests until 'extraordinary events jeopardize their supreme interests'. Further, both have called for "regular working level meetings to be held among all the nuclear powers to discuss issues of common concern". It suggests a welcome understanding between India and Pakistan to take the nuclear debate from the regional to the global level.

A report highlighting the immediate focus after the Conference on Confidence Building Measures (CBMs) and other specific recommendations of the CPG India-Pakistan Nuclear Danger Taskforce.

Chechen Refugee Camps.

Approaching winter of 2003 reports began to filter out from Helsinki Watch and other sources close to Chechnya, that Russian leader Putin planned to dismantle the Chechen refugee camps that winter and send them home to Chechnya. The obvious intentional cruelty of this potential action cannot be overstated. The Caucus winters can be as brutal as any on the Siberian steppes. Most of the Chechen homes in Grozny had been levelled and livestock were gone. To return civilians, children and elderly, with the clothes on their backs, through the winter elements to homes that didn't exist felt like Putin seeking vengeance on the stubborn Chechen independence movement.

We joined voices with several human rights organizations to protest and push to rescind the decision Putin was moving toward. Rather than target the UN, or US policymakers, we targeted other aid groups to join in a chorus decrying the proposed action. Most importantly, we reached out to the Russian government, to its foreign ministry and interior ministry to inform it that we were aware of its intentions and would decry it and publish it until international outcry stopped it. We pointed out the flagrant cruelty. We were pleasantly surprised when the order was cancelled. Russia indicated that they would break the camps down in the spring. The delay saved the elderly and infant exposure to deadly winter elements.

CHAPTER TEN: IT CONTINUES TODAY: D.R. CONGO, CENTRAL AFRICAN REPUBLIC, NIGERIA AND SYRIA.

D.R. Congo: Rape Capital of the World.
Central African Republic (CAR): Christian and Muslim Massacres.
Syria: Unlimited Cruelty and Genocide.

This book is about solutions for genocide and several examples are discussed but it is also important to mention what this book does not cover. It does not cover the South American massacres and genocide that occurred in Guatemala during the 1980s under the dictator Montt, and the massacres in Colombia at the hands of the FARC, ELN and AUC. The narco-terrorism and kidnapping that were the primary characteristics of the Colombian human rights abuse paled when compared to the civilian massacres from 2000 – 2004. In

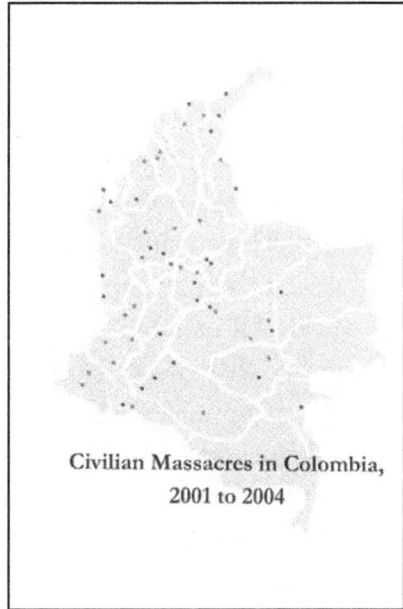

Civilian Massacres in Colombia, 2001 to 2004

addition, Chile and Argentina witnessed some of the worst South American dictatorships that 'disappeared' members of the opposition and other civilians. These also are not included here. The lives lost are no less precious.

In Africa, the terrible dictatorship of Nguema in

Equatorial Guinea that more than 50,000 dead in a nation of only 500,000 is an area of research that deserves more attention and study. The Tutsi massacres of Hutu in Burundi in 1972 and 1988 are historically overlooked and are crucial to understanding the cycles of violence between these two ethnicities. Without taking these into account, true healing cannot happen between the two. Mugabe's man-exacerbated famine of 2002 in Zimbabwe targeted political adversaries through starvation, plundered the resources of a nation and deprived whole generations of their potential.

In Asia, the horror of North Korea and the ideological genocide that has used torture and starvation as a tool against its own people is an ever present danger. The case for man-exacerbated famine as genocide was particularly strong in 1994 and 2002 as a series of classifications of its citizens according to perceived loyalty, allowed Kim Jong Il to callously claim that North Korea could lose $2/3^{rd}$s of its population and be stronger for it. It remains one of the worst human rights offenders in the world. All of the CPG reports on these areas are included on this book's website. Burma (Myanmar) has ethnically cleansed and marginalized its Karen, Shen, Mon and Rohingya minorities. Millions are displaced in a society where the military junta represses almost all freedom. In Indonesia, several areas experienced massacres: the Maduras in Borneo at the hands of the Dayaks, in East Timor during the movement for independence, of course, the Moluccas Muslims killed by Christians which prompted the Muslim Jihad against the Christians in Sulawesi discussed in the introduction. The two largest repressive regimes in Asia remain Russia and China. The repression of Soviet times, with its deadly purges of millions and political gulags, is over. But Russian President

Putin's use of intimidation and jail to quell political adversaries and critics represents a lighter version of repression that exists today. Critics of the regime have been assassinated and Russia continues to bully its neighbors Georgia and Ukraine by invading democratic Georgia and annexing parts of Ukraine and shutting off their gas in their harsh winter. Early in Putin's first term, he ordered the obliteration of Grozny during the war with Chechnya. While Putin's behavior is authoritarian and not genocide, it warrants attention. Today's bullies are tomorrow's genocidaires. China, while not as repressive as under Mao, or even Deng, continues to repress independence movements. Internet service in the Western Xinjiang province has been blacked out to restrict information about the restive Muslim province. Tibet has seen the 'sinoization' of its nation both through the mass immigration of ethnic Chinese to dilute the Tibetan population, and through the official restriction of Tibetan culture and language. This is a subtle form of genocide when a nation or ethnicity is slowly extinguished.

In summary of what this book is *not* about, there are few places in the world which have not seen massive human rights abuse, massacres or genocide in the past 100 years. I have covered the most impactful ones or the ones I had significant background information on. Many of these areas were reported on by the CPG and those reports are available on this book's website for you.

Lastly, this book does not cover femicide, an emerging concept in genocide prevention. In many places around the world, policies exist that encourage the abandoning of female children. These deadly and restrictive policies qualify women and girls as targets for genocide if they constituted a group in the genocide convention.

***

I have been writing some part of this book, on and off, since 1997, when I began writing my master's thesis at Georgetown University on indifference to genocide. My last rewrite occurred in 2014 and took almost a year as a Visiting Scholar at George mason University's S-CAR – now Carter School. Since I began writing the book, there is good news and bad news. The good news is that successful prevention strategies are beginning to be used more often. The Mass Atrocities Prevention Board, the Right to Protect Working Group, CSO and other Departments at US State and USAID, the UNOSAGP and the Great Lakes Conference on Genocide Prevention, as well as several schools and nonprofit organizations, are all undertaking steps toward early warning and prevention.

The bad news, though, is that throughout the twenty years from 2004 – 2024, since the CPG closed, genocide and massive human rights violations have not abated. Subsequently genocide has occurring in Nigeria, Syria, Central African Republic, Myanmar, and possibly in Nuba, and Darfur, Sudan. I no longer have a staff watching every hotspot in the world, but there are easily more than a dozen places that warrant close watching beyond those mentioned earlier: Syria, Iraq, Pakistan, Guinea, Niger, Yemen, Ukraine, Ethiopia Afghanistan, DR Congo, Turkey, Azerbaijan, Lebanon and Haiti.

D.R. Congo: Rape Capital of the World.

There has been some progress in eastern D.R. Congo in recent years. UN ground troop campaigns in eastern Congo in 2003 and 2007 have proved successful defeating and disarming rebel militias and keeping the peace during the past ten years. The disputing Hema and the Lendu have ceased hostilities, which were usually characterized by massacres. In late 2013, the vicious militia M23, considered a Rwandan proxy militia, was abandoned by Rwanda and the UN chased the vestiges of it from its last strong holds. Unfortunately D R Congo remains one of the most dangerous places in the world, especially for women. It is the 'rape capital of the world' with one woman being raped nearly every minute.[55] The perpetrators of rape were initially members of the assorted militias who were unchecked in their attacks on women.

Today, some of the perpetrators are members of the Congolese government army, whose ranks have been swelled by militias joining without the proper training in human rights and a code of conduct. The following are excerpt of interviews of some of these soldiers and details their justification for rape. Former Mai-Mai militia who were absorbed into the DRC army were interviewed about their practice of raping women. Each of the several men interviewed admitted to raping between two to twenty women.

Soldier One: "We know that it is not a good thing but what do you expect? We spend a long time in the bush

---

[55] www.stoprapeinconflict.org/dr_congo

and when we meet a woman and she will not accept us then we must take her by force."

Soldier Two: "It's all about control. Before raping them, I made sure that the women were in good health. Just by looking at her, I could tell if she was sick or not."

Soldier Three: "…Well, we were just abiding by the conditions of our magic potion. We had to rape women in order to make it work and beat the enemy."

Soldier Four: "For myself, I'm doing just like everybody else."

Soldier Number Two: "We raped as we advanced from village to village."

All except one soldier interviewed had a double standard, when asked if it would be okay if their sister or mother were to be raped by soldiers. [56]

Parts of eastern D.R. Congo are stable due to successful UN military peacekeeping missions. The most recent of these successes was the military defeat of the vicious rebel group the M23. However, women and children remain in constant jeopardy of being violated, often with irreparable injury, rendering the victim's incapable of reproduction and shunned by their family. Some die from the attacks.

---

[56] https://www.youtube.com/watch?v=ZbZIK9Ce0yM

Central African Republic (C.A.R): Christian and Muslim Massacres and a *Late* Response.

"Central African Republic is the worst crisis people have *never* heard of. "[57]

Samantha Power, US UN Ambassador

Central African Republic is the site of the world's latest genocide. After the overthrow of the unpopular despot Bouazizi, Seleka, the largely Muslim coalition of rebels that replaced him, could not be controlled by the coup leader Michel Djotodia. Looting and pillaging led to brutality and then wanton massacres of unarmed Christian civilians by the Seleka rebels. In November 2013, the ground situation had already led to thousands dead and tens of thousands fleeing. The tide of Muslim on Christian massacres began to turn with the advent of the 'Anti-Balaka' (anti-machete) Christian vigilante/rebel groups that began to massacre unarmed Muslims. By January 2014, Djotodia bowed to regional pressure and went into exile. The Muslim Seleka rebels began to fall apart and were unable to protect Muslim communities. As a result, there have been massacres against Muslims throughout the North, brutality is common and more than 8,000 Muslims remain trapped in Bozoum. 60,000 fled in two months, further destabilizing an

---

[57] http://www.theguardian.com/world/2013/nov/22/central-african-republic-verge-of-genocide

already very unstable region.[58] The 8,000 trapped Muslims are in clear danger. Both the Muslim massacre of Christians and the Christian massacre of Muslims are genocide. They each were intentional, habitual and clearly one of the primary characteristics of the ongoing abuse. 6,500 U.N and A.U peacekeepers currently deployed in C.A.R have been unable to curtail the violence or control the situation.[59] The remoteness of C.A.R, lack of early warning and lack of a standing rapid deploy force cost the few pivotal months that may have allowed for this force to have been effective. It does not matter how many firefighters one sends when the house is already burned down. The problems of mankind do not disappear as time passes, but they continue like time, seasons and everything else. Proactive work and resources need to be invested now to prevent the next generation of problems approaching down the road. We must be ready. These problems are coming, guaranteed.

[58] http://www.washingtonpost.com/world/africa/tens-of-thousands-of-muslims-flee-christian-militias-in-central-african-republic/2014/02/07/5a1adbb2-9032-11e3-84e1-27626c5ef5fb_story.html
[59] http://www.washingtonpost.com/world/africa/tens-of-thousands-of-muslims-flee-christian-militias-in-central-african-republic/2014/02/07/5a1adbb2-9032-11e3-84e1-27626c5ef5fb_story.html

Syria: Unlimited Cruelty and Genocide.

"How can you sit there and eat your dinner and go about your lives when they are killing us?"

Syrian Mourner on blog site

Consider Syria: over 130,000 souls have been lost to warfare and genocide over two years, with fitful international efforts to end the conflict. None of the major players, Russia, China, Iran, U.S., Saudi Arabia or the UN, seem to be acting with the necessary sense of urgency that these lives deserve. The failure to work effectively in late 2011 or early 2012 to prevent the Syria catastrophe means that over 7 million people are now affected, and an already volatile region is enflamed. After drawing a firm line, President Obama's tepid response to the massacres in Syria and the use of chemical weapons, has done little or nothing to end a horrible ground situation. Here are seven million more lessons that early warning and prevention would have been the best course of action.

Some genocide's have relatively straight forward fixes that can save lives. Whether we, as the international community, do anything about it is another story. Rwanda was relatively straight forward. Rewrite the UN mandate for its 2,000 troops already on the ground to include permission to use force to protect civilians, increase a stabilizing presence with thousands of additional UN or African Union troops, with armored personnel carriers, immediately and, of course, *call* it genocide. Bosnia and Kosovo, too, were relatively straight forward. As massacres and genocide were detected, NATO bombing commenced until peace was agreed upon. Even the complexities of the Holocaust had some clear-cut lessons: bomb the train tracks to Auschwitz and the gas chambers and facilitate the *Europa Plan* and heroes like Wallenberg with the means to save as many Jews as possible. Of course, recognizing Hitler's hate speech as dangerous and responding *before* there was a war, would have been the best response. There are, however, complex genocide's which do not offer an easy fix – Armenia was in a remote location and the genocide occurred during a world war without real warning. Ukraine's Stalin-induced famine also similarly occurred in a remote location, and in an area where there was no free press. Cambodia's genocide, also in a remote area, was an area with a recently reduced strategic interest. Most of these countries have little strategic interest to major economic players of the world, otherwise the urgency would be self-evident. Whenever governments, armed *with unlimited cruelty*, decide to victimize their own people, they can. The complexity, difficulty and international indifference conspire to assign a deadly fate. Consider the case of 130,000 unsuspecting Syrians.

Definitively, genocide has occurred in Syria. The U.N. Genocide Convention defines genocide as 'any of the following acts committed with the intent to destroy, in part or whole, a national, ethnical, racial or religious group (by) (a) killing members of the group." Syrian nationals have been targeted because they live in rebel stronghold areas. Massacres at the government's hands have occurred in Syria. The three standards held by the Center for the Prevention of Genocide when it was open have been met here:

1. *Is it intentional?* Clearly, these villagers were not caught in crossfire or accidentally gassed, so this is an easy yes.
2. *Is it habitual?* As the list of massacres indicates, yes, there are now dozens of examples of massacres at the government's hands including four UN-documented cases of the government of Syria using gas against its own people.
3. *Are massacres a primary characteristic of the abuse?* While there is torture and other mass atrocities present, the primary characteristics of the abuse are massacre, genocide and the internal and external displacement of people. This, too, is a simple yes. The UN Genocide Convention plus these three CPG standards makes this an iron clad yes. President Bashir al Assad is a genocidaire. Period.

The Syrian crisis began as part of the Arab Spring movement of 2011 to remove the autocratic Assad regime. When protesters and activists were killed and tortured, the movement grew into armed rebel action. A full blown civil war, massacres and genocide followed. The solution became geometrically more difficult and complex as the situation was allowed to run its course. The simplest and easiest time to intervene to prevent genocide was early during the Arab Spring. Pressure to transition the Bashir al Assad regime into exile or engage in the first steps of the process of democratization to a post-authoritarian government, should have been strenuously applied. As each month passed and the damage became permanent, different players from across the region entered the picture making a clear solution far more complex.

Today there is a slow-motion war in Syria which started as a popular uprising to unseat an unpopular despot. It has devolved into a regional conflagration that is slowly drawing in all of its neighbors. The quickest resolution to the Syrian catastrophe is that Bashir al Assad has to go, and quickly. Russia's Putin and perhaps Iran are in the strongest positions to exert influence on Assad's decision to step aside for the good of his nation. A national reconciliation government needs to begin the healing process and everyone else needs to go home.

CHAPTER ELEVEN: ENDING GENOCIDE PERMANENTLY.

Successful Interventions.
The Multi-Track Diplomacy Practice.
U.S Holocaust Museum Recommendations.
U.N. Early Warning and Rapid Response.
R2P. Aggressively Seeking Peace.
Amending the Genocide Convention.

"It always seems impossible until it's done."

Nelson Mandela

Successful Interventions.

There are several points during genocide when lives can be saved. The best known of these is heroism, which usually occurs *after* the danger has begun to unfold. It is, however, the least effective and most harrowing of preventative actions. Raoul Wallenberg, Andre Trocme, Oskar Schindler and Paul Rusesebegina, as well as other heroes of the world, are needed when the international community fails to prevent these man-made disasters from occurring. This reactionary, inconsistent effort will be the standard operating procedure of the world until we improve the other preventative types of action.

A second point at which lives can be saved is *as the danger begins*. When a life-threatening situation is starting to unfold, preventative action is absolutely vital. Many cases demonstrate this throughout the past one-hundred years: the

Armenians arming themselves at Musa Dagh and surviving, the Indian government sending Sikh police officers to serve as a buffer between the Hindus and Muslims and stopped the killing in Gujarat in 2003, and the UN-flagged French and Pakistani army missions to Eastern D.R. Congo which stopped massacres and defeated dangerous rebel groups in 2003 and 2007. These preventative missions, at the time when the situation is unfolding, are crucial until we develop better early warning and response systems. The impact of these missions cannot be underestimated. The lives saved are incalculable. Intervention is the second most effective approach. The world has begun to embrace this strategy more in recent years.

The third and the most effective way to combat massive human rights abuse is to anticipate and eclipses it *before* it begins. These life-saving actions almost never receive front page coverage. Rarely does a reporter file stories about a massacre that was prevented. But massacres and bloodshed which occur are considered newsworthy. It is human nature to take an interest in the sensational and not the mundane. Today, governments, non-government organizations and individuals, without fanfare or recognition, work on successful conflict preventative projects around the world. These programs receive a small fraction of the funding they need. Regardless, their cost is miniscule compared to the amount it costs to repair these human rights and humanitarian catastrophes after they unravel. The amount of money saved by early preventative action does not even begin to take into account the irreplaceable loss of life and human potential which is lost. In 2003, the Burundi election brought to the surface ethnic and rebel tensions similar to Rwanda in 1994. The danger of an imminent explosion in 2003 was obvious to most observers. NGOs and governments worked extensively to successfully defuse Burundi. Few outside of Burundi noticed. But this type of effort works. The US State Department prevention team worked on diffusing the 2014 Kenyan election results. The State Department's CSO Bureau is working to reduce the homicide rate in Honduras, to reduce tensions in Central African Republic and to attempt peaceful engagement in Syria. The countries of Norway and Denmark have human rights and humanitarian missions around the world, as does the E.U. Early intervention can diffuse volatile events and tensions and prevent the potential loss of life and mass atrocities. These strategies are being developed at foreign ministries, nonprofit organizations, Universities, and religious organizations around the world.

One of my favorite examples of a successful conflict prevention organization is the institution in which I wrote part of this book – George Mason University's Carter School for Peace and Conflict Resolution (formerly S-CAR). The Carter School has over a dozen missions around the world. It works in citizen diplomacy in the Caucuses, the Middle East, Asia, Africa, South America and locally. Students and graduates of this school are spread across the globe engaged in conflict resolution efforts. One is working in Burma to develop a Buddhist-based approach to conflict prevention among the groups. Others are engaged in track two diplomacy (citizen-diplomacy) and track one (government-diplomacy) between China and Japan regarding the disputed Senkaku/Diaoyu Islands. Their mission here is not to solve the conflict but to more clearly envision it and to clarify the differences. If the conflict is to be mediated or adjudicated by an international court, the research of Carter School will be a good starting point to clearly understand what the conflict is about. Another S-CAR project works to facilitate Syrian groups to meet together and attempt to envision a post-civil war Syria rebuilding process. Though the Carter School is one of the very earliest of such schools, several Universities now have schools and programs for peace and conflict resolution around the world. The Munk School of the University of Toronto, in Canada, is reputed to have a large monetary endowment – something that was unheard of twenty years ago. These programs yield tangible and intangible results, often beginning dialogues, methods and relationships that are pivotal to future successful peace efforts. But funding of conflict prevention, intervention and resolution work has lagged behind the field's rate of success and should be a priority if we are to move beyond the ever-repeating cycles of human violence.

Multi-Track Diplomacy – IMTD.

Ambassador John McDonald, Multi-Track Diplomacy Pioneer.

     The Institute for Multi-Track Diplomacy (IMTD) has been led by Ambassador McDonald for more than twenty years. It has worked on well over fifty projects worldwide. The approach is guided by innovation in the field of diplomacy:

'multi-track' diplomacy. The I.M.T.D expanded the diplomatic paradigm from only two tracks (government and citizen) to include seven more tracks. The additional tracks are professional conflict resolution practice, business, religion, education research and training, peace activism, funding, and media and public opinion. These have the potential to revolutionize diplomacy and conflict prevention and resolution throughout the world. Multi-track diplomacy acknowledges a larger, more complex picture of human interaction. It assumes that when countries, groups and entities have more connections with each other and understand each other better, they will be far less likely to engage in bloody conflict.   Jean Monnet used the 'business track' concept when he helped form the ECSC in 1951, which reduced tensions between Germany, France, Italy and the Benelux nations over the coal and iron ore resources in the ground. The reduction and disappearance of tariffs between these nations, and the joint ownership of resources fostered an era of economic cooperation which became the groundwork for the European Union. Today, the 27 nations of the EU are linked closely in a unique type of political and economic super-federation. These relationships were created on the bedrock of business and economic cooperation. This is a good example of the power of business diplomacy. There is another advantage of business-to-business track diplomacy. Nations and peoples who do business together often develop links with the local communities in which they conduct their business. In times of track-one (government) diplomatic stagnation, there are countless businesspeople whose self-interest makes them ideal for initiating other types of diplomatic ventures and outreach based on business relationships.

The 'religious track' has been a long standing vehicle for peace activism and dissent. Religious diplomatic activities can inform citizens and policymakers and curtail misinformation about perceived enemies with different religions. Religious organizations have a long history of peace-related activities during times of war and peace. This track acknowledges, as a fact, a track that has long been useful in both challenging preconceived notions and helping those victimized through man-made disasters.

The 'education, research and training track' is a quite large and innovative track of diplomacy. Educational student exchanges, classes, seminars, educational projects, and lecture series are some examples of educational-track diplomacy. Projects like those described at S-CAR, which are taking place around the world represent effective educational track diplomacy. Take the recent agreement between Israel and Palestine on shared water usage, a combination of citizen diplomacy and research diplomacy. IMTD was asked to mediate between technical experts on water, brought in from both the Palestinian and Israeli sides. After confidence building measures, each group wrote solutions where the two sides could collaborate. The similarities between the two proposals were the starting point of a relatively straight-forward agreement that is in effect today. Having the technical experts take the lead and design a mutually beneficial agreement based on research and science was something that politicians would not have been able to craft. The training aspect of this track is also fascinating. Just as the US Pentagon trains military commanders from around the world, IMTD and other organizations trains generals, politicians, business and other leaders drawn across civil society in the practice of conflict prevention, resolution and intervention strategies. After one class, the Colonel heading the Marines stationed in Iraq said to Ambassador McDonald: "We should have taken that class *before* we were deployed to Iraq. Do you know how many lives that could save?" While training leaders and citizens around the world in these practices is invaluable, it is rarely done due to the limited financial resources of these small NGOs. Another example of this is *peer mediation.* Consider the debate about gun control in the US. On one side people are very concerned about gun violence and death, especially among children victims at recent school shootings. On the other side, second amendment advocates believe that it is their inalienable right to protect themselves and to hunt. Both sides agreed at a recent debate in Washington, DC, however, that *peer mediation* is one of the best options to reduce gun violence in schools. IMTD, in conjunction with districts in the Maryland school system and in several other school districts around the US, trained entire schools in 'peer mediation and conflict prevention and resolution.' Rather than a small number of teachers, administrators and counselors trained, these schools now have hundreds of trained people, including all the students. The amount of conflict decreased in these schools dramatically because hundreds of trained eyes were better than a few.

'Peace activism' is another track of diplomacy, including protests and awareness-raising that are a staple of many democracies around the world. This type of activity has a long record of effectiveness. Peace activism has used art or even sports as an effective dialogue-initiating medium. In 2005, IMTD sponsored a sports tour of Indian and Pakistani soccer teams, trained in conflict prevention, to take a bus throughout the disputed region of Kashmir and play exhibition games with each other. This is just another strand in the web of peacebuilding that, together with other strands, can lead to substantive change. The 'funding track' of diplomacy includes 'carrot and stick' diplomacy. This involves nonprofits, private donors, international institutions, banks and governmental resources. It was used in Burundi in 2003. The promise of funding for various projects to various sectors helped keep the country stable after the results of the election were in.   Diplomacy through media and public opinion are fairly self-explanatory. As the media focuses more attention, and public opinion is informed on choices for peace over conflict and war, the public capital to will its politicians and leaders into making life-saving choices can be created.

Multiple approaches to diplomacy are essential in an ever-changing and complex world. Strengthening the strands of those in potential conflict serves to counterbalance the impetus to make war or break the peace. If Track One, government to government diplomacy struggles, there exist other options in the diplomatic tool bag which we must use.

In 1978 US President Jimmy Carter achieved a diplomatic success when he convened the Camp David Accords between Israel and Egypt. Before the meeting, the prospects for reconciliation after the recent war were poor. But in a salute to traditional diplomacy, Prime Minister Begin and President Sadat defied the odds and signed the Camp David Accords which remains in effect today. While a huge success, the result set an unrealistically high bar of expectation for future presidents and negotiators. These diplomatic sessions involve two political leaders who represent opposing viewpoints, who are pressured by their constituents to relinquish nothing and to gain everything that their side wants. They arrive at a highly charged environment in which failure is the default. But, in order to conduct a lasting treaty, compromise is required. Each side must give up something they cherish and face criticism and danger for the end result of peace. In Sadat's case, he was assassinated because of his compromise with the Israelis. Similarly, Israeli Prime Minister Rabin, who signed the Oslo

Accord with Yasser Arafat of the PLO was assassinated for his role in the peace process. It is a wonder that any of these sessions work. But occasionally they do. The Camp David Accords of 1978, the Oslo Accords of 1992, the Dayton Accords (Bosnian War) of 1995 are prime examples of this kind of success. The Comprehensive Treaty of Sudan of 2005 was distinct in that both governmental and non-profit organizations played major roles to end the conflict and encourage both sides to negotiate. But Track One Diplomacy is often a long shot. Hoping that the personal touch of an experienced hand can affect a successful resolution against the most daunting of odds, should not be the 101 plan of successful diplomacy. A better game plan and stronger long-term strategy relies less on personality and chance and more on having many strands of diplomacy working toward the same end goals at the same time. Thus multi-track diplomacy.

The better plan is to build the web of diplomacy through business, education, religious, training, research, peace activism, professional mediators, citizen diplomacy as well as track one – governmental diplomacy. This web of diplomacy geometrically increases the likelihood that a political climate at home will welcome the politicians negotiating and signing the final treaties.

I also have wondered if there are other undiscovered tracks of diplomacy. Are sports and recreation a form of diplomacy? Are women and women's groups another? Are non-profits and NGOs, such as IMTD different from track two? Do these links, currently labeled as citizen's diplomacy or educational diplomacy deserve study as possible new tracks? At an Ashoka-sponsored women's peace conference in 2001, there was a session moderated by an Israeli woman and a

216

Palestinian woman. Each one had suffered personal loss due to the conflict between the two peoples. At the end of a 90 minute very tense session, which included audience participation, the two women did something I was surprised to see. They looked at each other, paused and embraced and kissed with tears flowing. I could not imagine this happening at any other conference. This represents another potential track of diplomacy: gender diplomacy.

Building multiple strands of diplomatic bonds between peoples in potential conflict is the brilliance of multi-track diplomacy. The liaisons created bring a dynamic aspect to the very old field of diplomacy that is groundbreaking. The concept builds the process of diplomacy by strengthening the web existence of positive, productive, conflict preventing networks to serve as a bridge between conflicting nations and parties. Peace is more obtainable when these networks are built and embedded in daily life.

The crucial short term methods to end genocide are early warning and forecasting, political will and rapid response. The long term solutions include multi-track diplomacy, education, spreading democracy through civic building, and building a permanent national and international political constituency to help pressure policymakers. These practices will help end genocide and create foreign policies that reflect the values and morals of the individuals that comprise great nations.

U.S. Holocaust's Museum's Committee on Conscience's Blueprint for Genocide Prevention.

In 2008 the US Holocaust Museum came out with its *Blueprint for Genocide Prevention*. The committee was chaired by former US Secretary of State Madeleine Albright and US Defense Secretary William Cohen. It is brilliant. It provides a clear cut path to genocide prevention if policy makers and citizens are willing to walk it. If you don't have time to read the 100 page publication, read the four pages of recommendations. They advise everyone, from the US President to American citizens of their role and responsibilities in the solution. Core to their recommendations is treating genocide and genocide prevention with the importance and urgency it deserves.

The President is asked to raise the issue of genocide prevention to an NSC and comprehensive US policy level, spanning the methodologies of many US government agencies. President Obama fulfilled part of this recommendation by creating the Atrocities Prevention Board at the NSC which Samantha Power headed. The inter-department *Atrocities Prevention Board* spans the State Department, USAID, the Defense Department, other US agencies and several key NGOs. The two biggest drawbacks of this effort so far are its ineffectiveness and lack of transparency. Nonetheless, the APB exists and that is an important *start*. The blueprint also recommended that: the U.S Congress fund a Genocide Prevention Office, U.S foreign policy institutions to use preventative diplomacy, early warning, and carrot and stick diplomacy, de-escalation measures, and use military measures when the situation requires it. Lastly to build the international institutions and norms to respond to these threats.

The most urgent of all the recommendations is to create a Genocide Prevention Office. This is timely and crucial. The report estimated the cost would be $250 million per year to administer it. This is a very high estimate of costs. During our four years, the CPG never had a budget of more than $250,000 with a full time staff of six. We utilized fellowships, interns and volunteers. The CPG example is not a stable or permanent model because we were too underfunded and ultimately went out of business for lack of money and donations. Both models represent extremes of resources – the CPG had an extreme lack of them and the USHM has called for an extreme over-abundance of funding. Somewhere in between is a reasonable figure that could assure that these man-made disasters would be a rare occurrence and eventually disappear from human conduct. A permanent, nonpolitically affiliated, non-religiously affiliated genocide prevention center is long overdue and is in the world's interest to fund completely, immediately.

U.N. Early Warning and Rapid Response.

Aggressively Seeking Peace.

The United Nations, by its charter, is a passive organization. It was not envisioned to be aggressive or to sanction military involvement of its troops, except in a reactive, peace-monitoring role. There is much frustration that the UN can only provide reactive help with refugees or wounded. But as any nation or organization built on democratic principles and 'living documents' the purpose and vision of the United Nations has evolved as the need to protect vulnerable people has changed. Practical measures had to be taken to be more forceful and proactive. The ad hoc nature of each mission is part of the founding principles of the UN to protect against UN abuse. This inherently inhibits a quick response time for proactive intervention to prevent useless loss of human life. There are two specific steps that can be taken to address this. A well-trained, multi-national standing army should be maintained for surgical as well as full-scale involvement for the specific purpose of preventing genocidal or large-scale abuses of humanity. Both Boutros Ghali and Kofi Annan, former Secretary Generals of the UN, called for such a standing rapid deployment force for the UN, in order to better respond to emergencies as they escalate toward genocide. It is no longer sufficient to state that the will or political capital for an intervention does not exist, a mechanism must be created to insure that in the future, resources to save lives will be there regardless of the political climate strategic importance e of the victims or geopolitical relations between powerful nations.

220

In recent years, we have seen a transformation of the mandate language which defines UN peacekeeping missions to include language more conducive for military operations, with specific language allowing the "use of force" to protect civilian life. D.R Congo has benefitted greatly from this with successes in the field in 2003, 2007 and 2012 against militias that perpetrated mass atrocities. But the issue remains, that if there are Security Council members that oppose intervention for political reasons, how do nations seeking to help alter the ground situation to protect civilians?

The Responsibility to Protect.

In October 2005, the United Nations passed a resolution on the 'responsibility to protect civilians from war crimes, genocide, ethnic cleansing and crimes against humanity. It marked the first step the international community has taken to make the concept of early warning and rapid response a functioning reality. Together with the UN Secretary General's report on the Responsibility to Protect (R2P) in 2009, these are good pronouncements and declarations of intentions and ideals. Like the Genocide Convention of 1948, its impact is a question mark. On one hand, the UN is a living body reflecting the will and complexity of the peoples of our world, so this may very well be a first step in the institutionalization of that commitment to protect over time. It does begin to provide an international legal framework for UN General Assembly member nation action. On the other hand, without significant commitment to early warning and rapid response institutions, non-political trigger mechanisms and an ever-building consensus of political will to support these reforms, R2P will remain only a resolution, a declaration of principle. It also requires UN Security Council action, which is heart of the problem of failure to act.

U.N Early Warning Office: Three is not Enough.

I visited the United Nation's Special Advisor Dieng's Office for Genocide Prevention in 2014 . His staff of ten is assigned between himself and the 'Right to Protect' Special Advisor. I met with his office manager, a competent genocide scholar who had significant field experience. By the end of the meeting I understood that there was an early warning system at that office for genocide prevention and for a moment my heart sang. The office manager informed me that it had three people and my heart sank. The world is too big, there are too many massive human rights violations for three people to handle.

The early warning system that the US Holocaust Museum's (USHM) 'blueprint' envisioned does not exists anywhere yet. Though there are several noble efforts. For example the USHM's 'genocide prevention center' is an attempt to create a forecasting mechanism to predict the likelihood of genocide in various areas once enough data is collected. The effort employs part-time staff who work from home and seem to be brilliant at what they do. But this is not the early warning system the US Holocaust Museum envisioned in its blueprint.

Genocide Watch is a longstanding organization founded and run by Dr. Gregory Stanton, usually with one to two interns, which does significant work with its limited resources. Aside from generating accurate and timely warnings, Stanton was a prime moving force behind the creation of an alliance which pushed the USHM's blueprint with policymakers to help create the Atrocities Prevention Board. He never ceases in his work.

There are several other notable and respectable human rights organizations: Human Rights Watch, International Crisis Group and Amnesty International are among the better known and active ones. Their missions are not specifically attuned to genocidal activities, but to human rights and mass atrocities in general, though these areas overlap. The point here is that despite the specific need for one or several major organizations dedicated specifically to genocide prevention – there are practically none.

Rapid Response.

An essential part of ending genocide is having a rapid response team poised to intervene when the situation warrants. In the near future, the United Nations should create a standing armed force for humanitarian and human rights intervention. Other regional authorities can institutionalize their local cooperation to create a worldwide network for genocide prevention and mass atrocities rapid response. Organizations such as the African Union, North Atlantic Treaty Organization, the European Union, the Organization for American States and Economic Community of West African States, not to mention other regional authorities and alliances, a framework can be created for rapid response to genocides, mass atrocities and other significant man-made and natural disasters. While ultimate options for intervention currently rests with the Security Council, as with any democratic institutions, checks and balances must exist to allow for alternate action in case the Security Council fails to act. The implicit charge of the genocide convention is that failure to act during times of genocide leaves the UNSC culpable. Essentially, if one nation leader with a Security Council veto chooses moral indifference to genocide, the principles of 'right to protect', democracy, and our moral convictions are substantial enough to outweigh the UNSC protocol. The current R2P (Responsibility to Protect) discussion focuses on whether R2P redefines sovereignty in such a way that empowers other UN nations to intervene to preserve life.

When the UN Early Warning Office predicts genocide and unfolding actions and confirms unfolding dangers – it must inform a mechanism in the UN that triggers the UNSC or the General Assembly to action for the deployment of the pre-existing standing army with life-protecting "use of force" mandate language. Once the precedent and effectiveness become standard and routine, a large portion of human rights violations will decrease. It is the same simple concept of having an effective police unit poised and ready to respond to crime. Some of that crime will not occur when the consequences are known and immediate. While this does not solve the underlying roots of these conflicts, it certainly aids in reducing the human rights and humanitarian tragedies related to these man-made problems and crimes.

The standing force should be comprised of UN troops uniquely committed to the principles for which the UN stands and the applicable conventions. The mandate would be to secure the safety of those endangered by the genocidal activity, using any means within the scope of the international laws of war. This well-prepared force would prevent the need for international politicians to convince an involvement-wary audience at home, because no domestic soldiers would officially be put in danger. The UN soldiers would have a dual status, as citizens of their home nation and as soldiers of the UN.

Amending the Genocide Convention.

Another potential strategy to enable timely intervention when the UN Security Council is bogged down is to amend the Genocide Convention. When I returned to Washington, DC following a ten year absence, my old mentor and colleague Ambassador McDonald handed me a piece of paper and asked me: 'What do you think of this?' It read:

"State Parties to the Present Protocol

Considering that in order to further the purpose of the Genocide Convention and its provisions, it would be appropriate to make an exception to the principle of national sovereignty, as described by International Law and the United Nations Charter in particular; and allow the international community to intervene with military force in the territory of the state that fails to protect its own nationals who are targets of genocidal acts described by Article 3 of the Genocide Convention, entered into force January 12, 1951.

Article 1

A State party to the Genocide Convention that becomes a Party to this Protocol, recognizes the authority of the General

Assembly and the Security Council, to declare a situation occurring on the soil of any UN member state against its own nationals as, 'Genocide' according to the Genocide Convention, in particular Article 3, and the jurisprudence of international tribunals applying the Genocide Convention.

Article 2

In the absence of action by the General Assembly and Security Council, to an act of Genocide, a State Party to the Genocide Convention that becomes a Party to this Protocol acknowledges the right of the international community to intervene with military force to protect the nationals of a State in a case described in Article 2. Such actions shall not be considered a breach of the Principle of National Sovereignty as described in the United Nations Charter, and relevant norms if International Law, and shall respect the remaining relevant norms and principles of International and Humanitarian Law in particular.

Article 3

This protocol shall come into force when fifteen members of the UN general Assembly ratify it.

Proposed by John W. McDonald, U.S. Ambassador, (Ret.). Chairman and CEO Institute of Multi-Track Diplomacy"

This may well be another good concept for an end run around the UN Security Council when it is caught in paralysis and the people who are dying need swift response. A low threshold for coming into force (15 members) has precedent with the establishment of the International Criminal Court and would apply only to those countries that ratify it. Democracies are based on principles of checks and balances. As the world's largest democratic organization, the United Nations' executive leadership, the Security Council, should have balances built in that weigh world opinion, world morality, the emerging Responsibility to Protect and the spirit of the Genocide Convention against a flawed Security Council mechanism that allows one nation to veto and stop life-saving activities. This is one such tool to rectify this genocide-enabling oversight.

CHAPTER TWELVE: ENDING THE PHILOSOPHY OF INDIFFERENCE.
The Timothy Principle and the Total War Concept.
Creating Permanent Institutional and Political Will.
Internalize World Citizenship – Jean Monnet's Lessons.
Ending War through Democracy-Building.
Our Best Practices.
The Philosophy of Not Helping.
The Unfinished Recipe. The Missing Ingredient is You.

The TIMOTHY Principle and the Total War Concept.

"It wasn't necessary to use that awful thing."[60]

> General Dwight D. Eisenhower on
> using the nuclear bomb during World
> War Two.

To be effective in the prevention of genocide and crimes against humanity, international treaties must be binding and enforceable. They must have teeth. As the Armenians, Jews, Poles, Gypsies, Serbs, Bengalis, Tutsis and others were to find out, sympathy, and even the will to act, are often not enough. Aside from effective early warning, there need to be treaties, arrest warrants and mechanisms which can legitimately empower proactive human rights and humanitarian solutions.

---

[60] Peter Calvocoressi, *Total War*, P.83.

We have seen clear evidence of the power of the ICC's indictment with Sudan's al Bashir's curtailing of abuse in Darfur and allowing the South to break away. Without treaties and mechanisms with 'teeth,' perpetrators are unlikely to yield and are less likely to be defeated or stopped. *Treaties which are International Must Often Have Teeth to Yield results* – or, *TIMOTHY,* the Timothy Principle. The missions of the UN are done on an *ad hoc* basis. When an emergency arises there are two time-consuming stumbling blocks: the political will of the UN Security Council must be garnered, and then the actual physical resources must be made available. Transports may arrive from one nation, air coverage from NATO, and troops from several nearby states. Logistically, it is very difficult to coordinate these activities, not to mention deciding who is to pay the bill. This inefficient approach has caused immobility in several situations, unconscionable delays that indirectly lead to the death of thousands. This approach is further hampered by the indifference or intransigence of key players. However, when treaties, conventions and other mechanisms which empower enforcement have clear paths and consequences, the results improve when the 'teeth' in these mechanisms are explicit. Rwanda was a particularly good example of this inefficiency at the United Nations. Armored personnel carriers waited at a US base in Germany for deployment which was held up over a budget debate as an average of nearly 10,000 Tutsis perished each day. Treaties which are International must spell out consequences for both the perpetrators and the Security Council members who obfuscate in the face of deadly results. These members must be held accountable and, in a strict sense, legally liable for a failure to intervene in the most egregious types of human rights abuses. In determining this, a greater emphasis must be placed on the recognition of unfolding genocide through clear verifiable standards.

At the Center for the Prevention of Genocide, we used the UN Genocide Convention definition, but recognized ideological groups as potential victims as well. We emphasized three standards to answer the question of 'what is the magic number for genocide to have occurred?' Currently the number of 5,000 is loosely discussed as a potential standard for genocide in the mass atrocities prevention community. This arbitrary figure denies context and the preciousness of individual life. The CPG instead emphasized whether the massacre of unarmed civilians was *habitual*, *intentional*, and among the *primary* conditions of abuse. If these factors were all met we declared that genocide was taking place and required an immediate, vigorous response. Whether standards follow these conditions or any one of a number of potential conditions, it must be clearly defined and, when reached, trigger an automatic legally sanctioned response.

Punitive measures under modern international law are taking shape with the reparation rulings of several European nations on behalf of the persecuted Jews of the Second World War. Restitution of personal property, cultural property and territory has expanded to include the return of civilians to their hometowns in Bosnia and Rwanda. These are precisely the kind of teeth that international law must have in order to be effective.

In order to apply the *Timothy Principle* effectively and give teeth to international prevention, intervention and sanctions, it is essential that the UN trigger mechanism for issues of genocide is de-politicized. The UN Security Council naturally brings into its meetings the domestic and international policies of its member nations. But the political climate at home, during a given election year, should have no bearing on the Security Council's decisions to intervene in acts of genocide. It is no longer acceptable that one nation's domestic political climate can determine whether genocidal activities are acknowledged and halted.

The UN would not function properly without a Security Council. The veto of each of its member nations is an important 'check' against any nation dominating the Council. Conversely, if there is a standing UN force ready for humanitarian intervention, political vetoes of an action will decrease. This would be the 'de-politicization' of the UN Security Council's decision-making process regarding issues of dire humanitarian concern. If the main impetus for domestic politics to conflict with the Security Council is removed, then the danger it has posed in vital humanitarian interventions will lessen. Through the professionalization of the UN armed forces, Security Council members will have less face to lose if a peacekeeping or humanitarian mission goes wrong. The troops involved will be acting as citizens of the UN in humanitarian or peacekeeping instances alone. If the lens of nationalism is removed regarding these brave blue helmets, perhaps the significance of their UN mission will take priority over the significance of their home nation. If the resources are there, perhaps the proactive blue helmet humanitarian missions will find broader UN Security Council support.

***

The 'total war' concept should also be considered in as a component of genocidal activity. Few genocides have

231

occurred without being accompanied by war that often masks the severity of the civilian targeting. Since World War Two, there has been a growing historical trend toward the 'total war' theory's inclusion of civilian targeting. Not only is this a monumental step backward for humanity but it has also led to the political justification of genocidal conduct.

There are aspects of the 'total war' concept which warrant an expansion of the definition of genocide to include some conduct during wartime activity. Most wartime civilian dead and wounded are primarily considered under rulings concerning mass-atrocities or crimes against humanity, or a byproduct of the dangers of the war. But there is an aspect of genocidal conduct if the perpetrator is indiscriminately killing civilians without specific military objectives. Examples of this include the firebombing of civilian population centers during World War Two to the Syrian government 'barrel bombing' neighborhoods and entire cities in rebel controlled areas indiscriminately. The burden should be on the aggressor to justify the overwhelming targeting of civilians for a military goal.

The blurring of the line of military action specifically targeting civilians can be traced back to the Nazi blunder of the bombing of Rotterdam, Netherlands after it had just surrendered. Until May of 1940, both sides had followed relative international standards of warfare regarding the targeting of civilians in the theater of war. Civilians were not usually specifically targeted during military operations with the exception of two circumstances: the city where they lived housed a legitimate enemy unit or target or if the entire region had surrendered but this particular city was had not. When the Nazi's bombed Rotterdam, in what was a clear blunder, the

British responded with a blanket bombing of German cities. One wonders whether the gloves coming off at this particular juncture in the war making civilians 'fair game,' set the precedent for the horrible criminal activity of the Nazi regime crimes of the Holocaust.

Creating Permanent Institutional and Political Will.

There is no point to sending firefighters when the house has already burned down.

If a Congressman or woman were to assume a leadership role on the U.S House Appropriations Committee, they could help ensure a serious Congressional funding commitment to genocide prevention. Until that person arrives, or in case they never do, we as unelected citizens, will have to make the difference. We can help create a national and international constituency who believe in this issue and expect our policy makers and elected officials to work to fund these preventative strategies. Demanding 'best-practice' solutions of your government is not just an ideal, it is a right that you have and a responsibility you share if you agree with the premise of this book. Genocide and many of the other ills of humankind are preventable, but an investment in that process needs to be tangible and permanent.

The founding fathers of the United States created a Republic based on sharing power because we are all flawed and the risk for abuse is great. The US Constitution created a successful democracy, in part, because of the wisdom that assumes human nature includes bad behavior. The absolute corruption that goes with absolute power is an absolute part of human nature. This was recognized in the innate skepticism of man's unchecked behavior by many of the Eighteenth Century political writers. It was based on the tyrannical behavior of King George III toward the American colonies. Many of the pilgrims and settlers of the colonies left the countries of their origins because of the oppressive role religion played in their home governments, rendering them outcasts. To break away from those oppressive conditions elsewhere, the American founding fathers sought a 'balance of power' between the Executive and Legislative branches of government with the Judicial Branch aiding with additional oversight and powers. Religion and state were separated lest the abuse of religious minorities occur in the new American nation. The First Amendment in the Bill of Rights allows the individual to defend himself from the corruption and cruelty of individuals and governments through the balancing powers of freedom of speech, assembly and press. If great democracies are built with these protections in mind *against* the worst characteristics in man, should we not make the same assumption in the democratic community of nations? Should we not protect ourselves *against* the worst characteristics in man, on the world stage?

The knowledge that mankind can be evil helps democracies to protect themselves with checks and balances. We need to assume, similarly about leaders and characteristics of leaders throughout the world, so that when the next Adolf Hitler, Joseph Stalin, Pol Pot, or Omar al Bashir appears, there are measures to keep them in check. On the international level that means early warning to predict and detect when that inevitable part of human nature rears its ugly head. It also means having a rapid deploy force at the ready to intervene when evil thought becomes evil deed. Becoming a person who believes in this and will stand for these protections at the international level is the beginning of a constituency of one.

***

Some children have imaginary friends. When I was a boy, I had an imaginary planet - called Jenoco. I wrote the history and treaties, drew maps for years of my childhood. When entered boarding school, it was time to end Jenoco and put childish things aside. I wanted to conclude Jenoco in a way that the imaginary planet would live in peace. It ended when a federation was created that allowed any nation to join if they were committed to three things: democracy, nuclear non-proliferation, safe and clean environmental practices. This Federation, 'the Green States,' grew until more than 70% of Jenoco was part of it and this heralded in a period of long uninterrupted peace. As childish as 'Jenoco' may have been, there were some assumptions which I took for granted for peace. Democracies do not fight democracies is one such assumption which is true.(see the statistician RJ Rummel's work). The European Union today has the 'feel' of how I envisioned 'Jenoco.' Democracies functioned in a way that their people could go about their lives trying to enjoy their friends and family and make a living. Ending genocide, famine, preventable disease and conflict is not as daunting a task as we may think. As with most things, the most difficult part, really, is getting started. In centuries and millennium from now, will we still be struggling with the same problems that plague us now? Will the history of humanity be long periods of struggle, briefly illuminated with periods of democracy and peace, only to fall back into periods of darkness? Or will we learn from our mistakes and finally push away from our long periods of warfare and genocide by developing perpetual democracy and perpetual human rights protection?

***

When a teacher imparts the lessons of conflict and genocide prevention to a class of eager minds, or when an author finishes a book on genocide prevention, these are acts which attempts to build a national and international constituency for this type of belief and work. There is today no real genocide-prevention lobby. Sometimes outraged relatives or human rights activists may lobby congress with varying degrees of success to change other nation's policies of repression and killing. What real power does the Nuba lobby have, or the Northern Nigerian lobby? What power do the Syrian victims' lobby wield in the hall of Congress? About as much as the Tutsi, Acholi, Hema and Lendu lobbied did before them during their massacre – practically none. In recent years, we have seen the rise in popularity of *Save Darfur* and other similar national nonprofit organizations that raise the awareness of millions of people on an issue of suffering which they were previously unaware. In an age of crowdsourcing, crowd funding, Twitter, Facebook and YouTube, the possibility of building a collective consciousness of a people on an issue is as great as ever. To help people realize and internalize their refusal to accept massive human rights violations as business as usual is possible today more than ever.

Take Norway for example. This nation of five million does more to combat human rights violations around the world, per capita, than any other nation. Denmark and Sweden are close behind. These nations have internalized their commitments at an individual level and a national political level in support of human rights and it is a very cornerstone of their foreign policy. The US briefly considered human rights as a cornerstone of its foreign policy under the Carter Administration. When this awareness permeates the national consciousness again and an urgency is built to permanently change our foreign policy – the global impact will be significant.

Ending War Through Democracy-Building.

Since the 1920s, the United States and American organizations have been sending civic-building associations to South America, to aid in building the backbone of democracies. The U.S has, to be sure, also been responsible for its share of coup d'états, supported dictators and pillaged natural resources in South America and elsewhere. But American-sponsored civic building associations and those organic to South America have, however, borne fruit in the past twenty years. Today, almost all of the governments in South America are functioning democracies with democratically elected governments, successful opposition transition in the position of President, freedom of speech, assembly and press with functioning checks and balances form other branches, Venezuela notwithstanding. There was hardly a time in the past Century when there were

237

more than two or three functioning democracies in South America at one time. Civic building associations and democracy movements work – they just take time and several attempts.

The rise of democracies in Africa and Asia is a long and bumpy road. The glorious flash of the 'Arab Spring' of 2011 – 2012, shows that the will for freedom is universal and stirring underneath even the strongest authoritarian governments. The fact that the wave of revolution failed to immediately create democratic governments is not surprising. The military in Egypt, for example, rightly deduced that the civic building associations were helping cause the undercurrent of democratic movement. They closed them all and jailed their leaders. These authoritarian regimes had been strictly curtailing the development of civic-building associations. Over time, as political parties are legalized, and unions and business organizations develop the backbone of civil society, reforms will take place which will give democracy a better chance of survival.

Inherent to well-functioning and mature democracies is the protection of minorities through the court system and the authority and power of the government. When the world is filled with functioning, stable democracies, the vehicles will exist to mitigate conflicts and strife's that have typically led to genocide and mass atrocities. When added to those stable governments are international early warning and rapid response systems for when an occasional situation gets beyond a government's control, then the world will be well on its way to ending genocide in human conduct. As democracies do not fight democracies, nor do they commit genocide.

Internalize World Citizenship: E.U Founding Father Jean Monnet's Lessons.

The European Union was the brainchild of Jean Monnet. He served as the Deputy Secretary General of the League of Nations when he was thirty-one years old. During World War Two he helped coordinate logistics for the transport of war materials from the US to Europe. He was also involved in the Marshall Plan in Europe after the war. After spending much of his life dedicated to assisting Europe after the two world wars, Monnet established some ideas about how to stop the countries on the continent from fighting each other again. One of the underlying keys to Jean Monnet's success in Europe becoming the EU was his assumption that nations that did business together, and had to share resources, would not fight wars with each other. The ECSC founded in 1951 put traditional enemies Germany and France (with Italy and the Benelux nations) together on the same economic path by internationalizing the steel and coal in the ground in those nations requiring joint management of it. Eventually this led to the dissolving of tariffs and taxes, and essentially the creation of an economic free enterprise zone. If you lived in any of the member nations, you could own property or businesses in any of the other member nations without punitive tax consequences. This union gradually expanded to include other members and to become one political union. In 1993, the Maastricht Treaty laid out the structure of a European Super-State, a pseudo-federation with a unique executive and legislative structure, based on cooperation rather than competition. With the Euro and coordinated banking, trade, labor and commerce policies, a true super structure became to evolve where none had existed before. This was the framework for the European Union. Today it is both an economic and political union with 28 members, and has transformed the way a continent approaches business, quality of life and efficiency. None of these nations have fought in any kind of war or conflict against each other, while a member, during the EU's existence. They share a currency, economic and political cooperation, a no-visa border and a vision for the future of which few countries can boast. Monnet knew that this type of transformation of Europe would have to be gradual, so gradual it would hardly be noticeable at first. Over time, even the most fiercely proud nationalists came to associate themselves with their home nation and the greater EU. They have *internalized* their EU citizenship.

People unconsciously internalize many concepts. We are socialized to behave in certain ways, and we internalize those behaviors as part of the package of our identity. For example, four hundred years ago, if we asked a person 'what are you?' Their answer would likely be 'I'm an Alsatian, I'm Christian. I'm a villager. A farmer. A father, A daughter' Today we have expanded these categories to include the larger idea of our nationalism. Even during the fragmentation of Yugoslavia, when the combatants had been separated and plebiscites taken, 15-25% of the population polled considered themselves to be Yugoslavian. They had internalized this Pan-Slavic idea and remained committed to it. When people immigrate to a country, after a number of years, they sometimes begin to feel like members of the new nation in which they live. Sometimes it takes a generation or two before the child internalizes the new identity of the adopted homeland. But people can accept more than one identity. We see a clear example of this in the EU during its embryonic stage. People are both members of their nation as well as members of this newly expanded community. America provides another clear example. Anyone could be an American because, by definition, it is made up of a various of ethnicities and mixes. When one internalizes one's American-ness, it is the adoption of a set of ideas, principles and culture.

So too must we internalize, over time and generations, our world citizenship. We may not become like the 'green states' of 'Jenoco,' but we can learn to picture ourselves as citizens of the world, with responsibilities to people beyond our kin, ethnicity, religion and nationality. Just as Europeans 'internalized' Monnet's concept of a greater European, so too can we internalize an identity as a world citizen, with all the responsibilities and horizons that it implies.

Our Best Practices: Genocide Prevention, Conflict Prevention, Disease Prevention and Famine Prevention.

In the 2010s, when Fortune 500 companies had problems, they needed to solve, they called the professionals. Organizations like Gallup, the Corporate Executive Board and the Corporate Advisory Board paid large fees per year just so corporations could be members and have access to their databases and staff. When a senior vice president of a division of one of these large successful companies has a problem that is keeping him up at night, his first call when he goes into the office is often to one of these organizations. He/she describes the problem – marketing, layout, rollout, integration, software, labor, downsizing, production and so forth – whatever the problem, usually the 'best practice' staff representative replies 'no problem, we have you covered, I'll call you back soon.'

What happens next is a marvel of modern business. The lead staffer in charge of that client gets his team together and they research comparable situations in their database that other companies went through. Sorting through the specifics, they determine which solution is the industry-best solution and is applicable to their clients' needs. They learn the solution, fly out and teach it to their client. This can save clients millions of dollars and months, even years of headache and chaos. Using the best solutions that someone else has already used and is a proven winner; it is a no-brainer.

I have always hoped that government would function the same way. Why reinvent the wheel? If there is a department, an administration, an urban area, an authority that has brilliantly solved a situation similar to one unfolding elsewhere, shouldn't that database be available? In human rights, conflict prevention, resolution and intervention, there exist best practices too. Much of this intellectual capital, however, is being lost. For example, Ambassador McDonald, about whom much in this chapter is written, died in 2019. He worked every day until his mid-nineties. But when the Ambassador died, there will be incredible institutional memory loss. Organizations that undertake best practices for these norms should be captured so that their lessons learned do not have to be re-learned in the future, and at the cost of thousands or millions of lives.

The Philosophy of Not-Helping.

Which is the Philosophy and Purpose of America: Self Interest or Idealism?

During the five years of the Johnson Administration, the embers of JFK's idealism were visible with the Civil Rights Act, the Voting Rights Act, the Great Society and the War on Poverty. During the following U.S President, Nixon's term, his foreign affairs philosopher, and National Security Advisor, Henry Kissinger espoused and led a realpolitik philosophy based on the self-interest of the U.S. This policy has remained the platform from which almost all U.S. Foreign Policy emanates.

The philosophy of realism was clearly embraced by the ideals of the 1980s-1990s as it was to be known as the 'me' generation. Both liberal and conservative administrations assumed the realpolitik Kissinger concept of 'self-interest', as the guiding principle of the nations' foreign policy, has become elevated and is now perceived as standard and neutral, despite its bias toward one end of the foreign policy political spectrum. Because realism is perceived as neutral, it is difficult to recognize its dangers. But the politics that appeals primarily to self-interest loses the great benefits that come with attempting to improve our world. The joy of a child receiving gifts eventually graduates to a joy of giving to others – usually with your own children. But the benefits of a nations' policies of altruism are geometrically greater. Even today when the U.S State Department considers human rights, it must be considered in the context of our national security interests. The underlying morality of most Americans is not reflected in our foreign policy. While U.S. foreign policy does aid in the service of human rights, it is often done in spite of our moral belief system, not because of them. The undergirding of most of US foreign policy is realpolitik-based. Every recent President's foreign policy has asked the question first 'is engagement there in our self-interest,' when the question of greater value is: 'is human life at stake?'

The world interest is the American interest. Since Kissinger's realism guided U.S of U.S. foreign policy, the viewpoint has held sway ever since. The evidence that realism trumps idealism, regardless of party, can be seen in the failures to act across party lines in Rwanda, Darfur and Nuba, Sudan, D.R. Congo and recently in Syria, C.A.R and Nigeria. None of these areas or nations hold a strategic interest for the United States, but the moral imperative to end the suffering is as compelling as any.

When President Kennedy was assassinated in 1963, hundreds of millions mourned for the loss of a youthful, inspiring leader, but many also mourned the loss of something less tangible; they mourned the loss of idealism. President Kennedy inspired Americans and people throughout the world to dare to dream for a better world.

The elevation of this Kissinger philosophy of self-interest, and its adoption by all presidents who have followed Nixon represents a defeat of Kennedy idealism. Because self-interest is perceived as the cornerstone of foreign policy, it remains unseen, elevated and perceived as neutral. It is not neutral. It has not served my country - the United States, or the world it sometimes protects, well at all.

The idealistic proponents of America argued for better

outreach to teach fledgling democracies the best practices of building a successful democracy. We missed that opportunity when many of the Soviet Republics left the Soviet Union for independence, including Russia itself. Those years of transition from the USSR, to the CIS, to today offered several years of opportunity for the US and the West to play a pivotal role in helping Russia use, and then develop, the training wheels of their democracy. We failed to do this effectively because it was 'not in our strategic interest.' As a result, Russia today is still an authoritarian regime, and remains an active threat in international relations and, ironically, an indirect threat to American interests worldwide.

We failed to reach out throughout the Middle East during the Arab Spring, to aid the cause of democracy. We could have provided aid, advice, training, education, workshops, conflict prevention strategies and the best constitution thinkers and writers from around the world. We should have done that because it was the right thing to do. It also would have been the prudent thing to do in the long-term interests of a peaceful, democratic world. We should help each of these potential countries in transition to help frame these early nations' democratic aspirations in a structure that works, or in one whose principles would give it a good possibility of working, if their people so willed it.

Syria, Nigeria, C.A.R, and D.R. Congo all have human rights failures which would have benefitted from American effort and leadership. After Rwanda's genocide the lesson was clear that early intervention *was* in our self-interest. The fact is, early warning is always in our self-interest because *the world's self-interest is the American self-interest.*

If we do not take on a national responsibility to protect

those in danger, most of these problems will continue, and, more often than not, worsen. The EU is currently taking the lead in much of the preventative and response work in human rights. Russia and China should not be counted on to help and few nations have the resources to be as impactful as the U.S. does.

Is America the nation Kennedy inspired in us when he asked us for selfless sacrifice? Have our policies become too much the product of the realpolitik philosophy of pragmatic leaders who lack the vision and courage to act with urgency to create the world of which we dare dream? That debate is worth having. In the end, by embracing idealistic behavior in US foreign policy, the question becomes moot because promoting democracy and protecting human life is always in our long term self-interest.

Proponents of strict 'self-interest' and realism should concede that in an ever-connected world, the health and welfare of the world community is in our strategic interest. This is not only true because our citizens are from everywhere in the world, nor because we compete for trade partners on the entire world stage, but because the freedom we represent is universal. It is why we are often considered the indispensable nation. The fact that we have failed to act with any discernible urgency in many human rights emergencies does not negate that American ideals are rooted in principals of morality, fairness, freedom and equality. But the greatness of a nation lies in acting on those ideals. The hallmark of freedom is ethical treatment of others. Our Founding Father's assumed the worst in human nature and created a government that attempts to protect against our darker nature, it is a self-evident truth that aiding others in dire need fulfills this.

If the next Century is to see the U.S. continue its role as the world's 'indispensable nation,' it will not be because the U.S is the wealthiest, or the strongest or has the biggest economy. There have been scores of powerful nations, kingdoms and empires which no longer exist. Wealth ebbs, large militaries bankrupt nations and economies crash. Our indispensability is intrinsically tied to our place as the foremost democracy. What is the point of promoting freedom if the freedom we promote is brutal, mean and indifferent? During the Cold War, the U.S. and many of her allies stood for liberty. In the times to come, can the U.S. continue to be a nucleus of democracy-building *and* an indispensable force for human rights, not when it's convenient, not when the world is looking, but as a permanent part of its foreign policy. We should do this in a way that is not paternalistic, materialistic or chest-thumping. It would be fitting for a great nation and a world leader

■■

An Unfinished Recipe – the Missing Ingredient is You

"If we did all the things we are capable of, we would literally astonish ourselves."

Thomas Edison

In January 2010 an earthquake devastated the Caribbean Island nation of Haiti. The first private plane to arrive in Haiti from the west coast of Florida after the January 2010 earthquake was organized by a sixth grader at Out-of-Door Academy in Sarasota. She asked her father if his company plane would transport medical supplies if she organized it and he agreed. There are thousands of examples of young people starting organizations that save lives, help others in need or just make the world a better place to live. Three years ago Jane Evers, former first lady of Bradenton, Florida, established a charity called F.E.L.T – Feeding Empty Little Tummies. She had heard that the number of Manatee County children going hungry had exploded as a result of the recession. The organization grew until children at several elementary and middle schools were supplied with food as well as their families who were also experiencing hunger. Jane died of cancer on New Year's Eve 2014. Three days before she died, she was still running the organization, determined to ensure empty little tummies were filled. They continue to be filled today. The Emperor Augustus said that a leader should die on his feet running his empire and Jane practically did; she died as she helped others. There is not an age, or a place, or a circumstance, where you cannot make a positive impact or your surroundings and, indeed, even the world.

When I was twelve years old my mother gave me a book, *The Autobiography of Malcolm X* and I enjoyed it from the beginning because he wrote the book directly to you, the reader.

This book is written to you, the reader, for you to use. It is written by me, the author, but it is the story of tens of millions of people. *In Case of Genocide – Break Glass* is not just a story of our reaction to the massacre in Sulawesi, Indonesia, it is not just a collection of stories and histories of genocide over the past 100 years. It is *a call to arms* to you. When you hear of genocide, whether close to home or in far off lands, whether its people who are known or unknown to you, do whatever is in your power, and whatever is in your potential to end it. Whenever there is genocide, treat it like the emergency that the lives it is taking deserve. In case of genocide, break glass.

Epilogue

I sat on the porch thinking about the CPG and what we had accomplished. I was proud that the St. Petersburg Holocaust Museum was interested in our archives to possibly tell our story. I pushed past the laziness of the warm Florida day and went back inside, crouching to pull boxes of the CPG archives out of the small gnome-sized closet. After searching through the boxes, I found the two card organizers I had kept from the charity's contacts. I wanted to find out if we had been helpful to the Darfurians. My friends and I had just watched the US Presidential debate the night before and both candidates mentioned their commitment to ending the horror in Darfur, Sudan. Both called it genocide. I did not know with any certainty whether any of the publicity, reports or even the introductions we made for the Darfurians proved to be of any use.

"Hello, is Yusef of the Darfurian Community in Exile there?"

"Yes, yes, Richard, is that you?"

"Yusef, how are you?"

"Much better. Boy, am I glad to hear from you Richard. We tried to contact you to thank you. We emailed you and mailed you but everything just kept coming back."

"Sorry about that Yusef. When we closed, I just wanted to get away from human rights work for a while. I was burnt out."

"Really?"

"Yes," he continued, "you know Richard, we all sat down about three months ago and thought that if you hadn't come out and called it genocide in the months before you left. If you hadn't had that march and brought us together to meet those people – we would never have the gotten coverage we have now. Nobody would be calling it genocide. You know Rich, you really got the ball rolling and we wanted to thank you."

After we hung up the phone, I made the firm decision to write this book. It is not really about the wonderful volunteers we had or the work we undertook, it is really about how the human spirit can overcome indifference, lack of resources and evil conduct through will and perseverance. And that deserves to be shared.

I wish this book could have been solely about life-affirming stories of heroism. Perhaps that will be the next book. But the fact is, today if you live in a country where bad militias, armies or governments dislike you and trouble is coming to your door - run, flee, hide or fight, but do not wait for your rescue – there is no one coming to help. Not until people like you reading this book, and I, change that. This is the reality. There is no international super-structure designed to specifically respond to these areas where the need is greatest but the importance to powerful nations is negligible. This is what need to be corrected. That is the 'call to arms' of this book. Let's demand a system that changes this complete moral blind side of the world community.

My father once wrote about his hope for future generations:

"Thirty generations hence, I hope our golden, god like children look back at us with compassion and generosity, from a vantage point of an enlightened perspective and a profound maturity, and know, that in spite of all our fears, frailties and inadequacies as we beheld the awesome universe, some of us wanted to give them the stars, with love."[61]

In that spirit, let us create a world that is genocide-free. Let that be our gift to the next generation and the generations that come after them.

---

[61] *It's Like This Jim*, 1972.Copyright John J. O'Brien

Author in 1998 in Geneva, Switzerland at 32, where
the first chapters of Break Glass were written.

Author on a Creative Loafing magazine cover for the CPG's work on Sulawesi, Indonesia.

ABOUT THE AUTHOR

Richard O'Brien was raised in Toronto, Canada and Sarasota, Florida. He is a product of Culver Academies, American University and Georgetown University and wrote much of this manuscript in 2014 as a visiting scholar at (S-CAR) now the Carter School, at George Mason University. As a teacher, he instructed classes in *International Human Rights*, *Conflict in the Modern World* and *World Ideologies* at the University of South Florida and *World History, Women's Issues, American History, Geography and U.S Government* at the Duke Ellington School of the Arts in DC. A writer and human rights activist, he founded The Center for the Prevention of Genocide (CPG) from 2000 – 2004. The CPG actively worked to intervene and prevent genocide, massacres, human rights violations and starvation in in the following areas: Sulawesi, Indonesia, Nuba, Sudan, Darfur, Sudan, Chechnya, Colombia, Ituri and N. & S. Kivu, D. R. Congo, Uganda, Burundi, Zimbabwe, and Gujarat, India. During its existence the CPG also fielded a lecture series, a TV series, a yearly journal, more than twenty human rights reports and an India-Pakistan Nuclear Conflict Warning paper. By the time of its closing, the CPG had an office staff of 25 employees, interns, fellows and volunteers and a network of more than 700 individuals in hotspots worldwide.

His human rights work has been featured in Business Insider and on the cover of Creative Loafing, he has been published in the Washington post and the New York Times, interviewed on National TV and NPR and has given testimony in Congressional Sub-Committee and at the U.N. Subsequently, he has authored *Women Presidents and Prime Ministers*, 2017, 2018 and 2024 editions and has a TED X lecture on the same subject. He calls the DMV and Florida his home, and is the proud father of twins, Annalise and John A.C. O'Brien.

JENOCO PUBLISHING www.jenoco.org
Jenoco Publishing publishes works in human rights, women's issues, fiction and non-fiction and the twenty plus unpublished manuscripts of the O'Brien family.

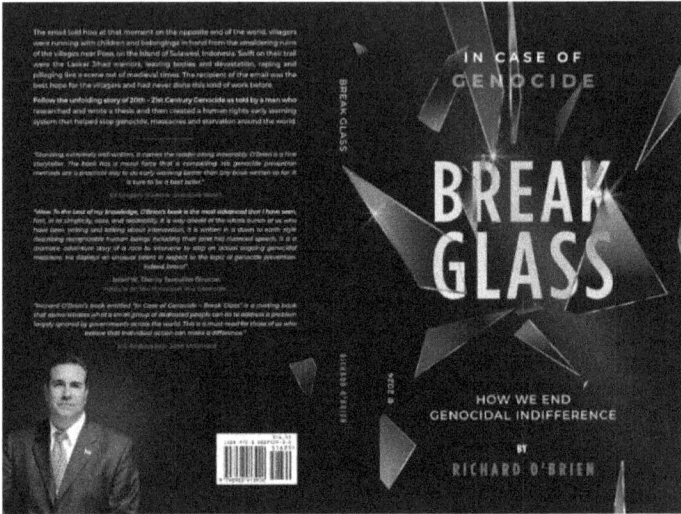

Experience the most harrowing stories of 100 years of genocide and a group of students who prevent it. $19.99 Abridged. 258 pages.

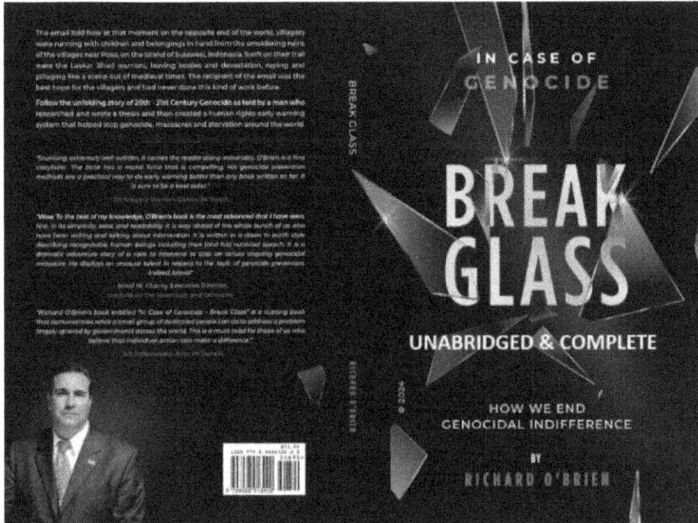

The Unabridged version features 200 additional pages, a 'how to' manual on how to create a human rights early warning system. $34.99

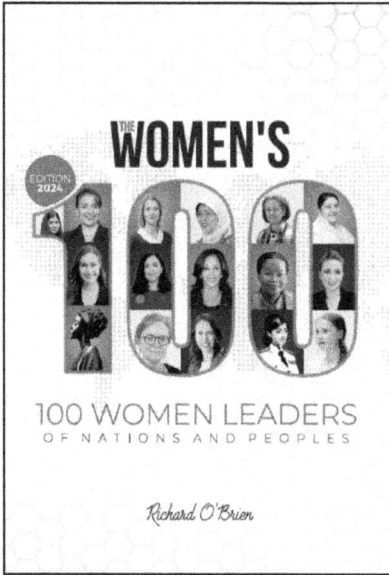

The Women's 100: 100 Women Leaders of Nations and Peoples

By Richard O'Brien

Meet the more than 100 women who have served as President or Prime Minister of their respective countries around the world and learn the stories of their adventures, struggles and accomplishments.

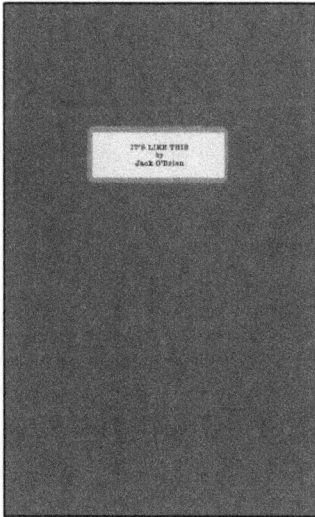

It's Like This

By Jack O'Brien

Ecclesiastic muralist and President of the Canadian's Writer's Guild John (Jack) O'Brien lived his life to the fullest, a lifelong deep love, the horrors and camaraderie of war and his art. He has taken his artist's pallet to put you on the battlefield, in the bedroom and in his mind. $14.99 Poetry. Vivid imagery.

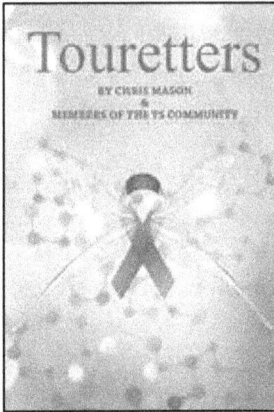

Touretters. This rare collection of 30 autobiographical stories written by parents and individuals who are living with TS. This book helps demystify the condition and touch your heart.

Non-Fiction. $19.99 Vivid imagery and language.

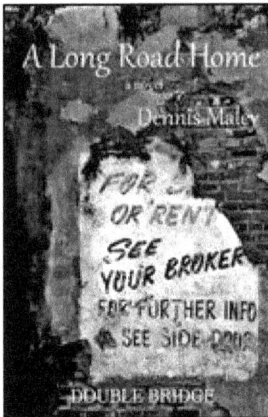

A Long Road Home By Dennis Mitch Maley.

After losing her mother to cancer, 22-year old aspiring singer Jenny Harris couldn't be more alone. Enter T.K. Connolly, a debauched recluse of a writer who is revealed as her biological father. Thet share a journey of self-discovery in the South. Fiction. $19.99

Matthew Mejia's TheFEEL marks his first book of poetry and is raw, powerful and vulnerable. Featured in Southern California College literature classes as an emerging talent.
Poetry. $15.99

www.ingramcontent.com/pod-product-compliance
Lightning Source LLC
Chambersburg PA
CBHW032052020426
42335CB00011B/306